WALKS THROUGH HISTORY
BIRMINGHAM

WALKS THROUGH HISTORY
BIRMINGHAM

John Wilks

DB PUBLISHING

First published in Great Britain in 2008 by

The Breedon Books Publishing Company Limited

Breedon House, 3 The Parker Centre,

Derby, DE21 4SZ.

This edition published in Great Britain in 2012 by The Derby Books

Publishing Company Limited, 3 The Parker Centre, Derby, DE21

4SZ.

ISBN 978-1-78091-176-2

Printed and bound by Copytech (UK) Limited, Peterborough.

Contents

amazon.co.uk®

A gift note from Ben Griffin:

Happy walking!! Love you lots xx From Ben Griffin

Gift note included with **Walks Through History: Birmingham**

Introduction

Walking through historic Birmingham

On a walk around the centre of Birmingham today the first impression you get may well be of a modern city, but there is history to be seen at every corner. Birmingham is a city with a rich and varied past. It has existed for over 1,000 years and in that time has grown from a tiny Saxon hamlet into Britain's second city. The Reformation, the Civil War, the Great Reform Bill, the Blitz; Birmingham has experienced them all, and they have all left their mark on the city. As the Industrial Revolution got under way, Birmingham became the leading industrial city in the world, and throughout the late 19th and early 20th centuries it was among the world's leading manufacturing centres. Examples of this industrial past and the civic pride it engendered can be seen all around, if only you know where to look.

All too often we walk around our cities with our eyes shut. We are so intent on concentrating on where we have to get to, so caught up in the bustle of city life and in so much of a hurry to reach our destination, that we forget to look about us. The aim of this book is to help the reader understand the history of this great city. Take the time to walk slowly around the city, following routes you do not normally follow, and look around. Walk through history and discover the past that is present on every street corner.

The walks

This book contains 12 walks within the city of Birmingham. Each walk covers a specific period in the history of Birmingham, and goes past historic buildings and other sites from that period. Together the 12 walks cover all the major themes in Birmingham's history, and if walked and read chronologically they lead the reader from Birmingham's humble beginnings in Saxon times to the present day.

Getting to the walks and doing them

Birmingham has a very compact city centre. Six of the walks in this book are around the centre, and each starts from an easily recognisable landmark. The centre is easily covered on foot, and all of the starting points are easy to find. The other six walks are in the suburbs, and for convenience each starts from a railway station within easy reach of the city centre. Birmingham is fortunate in having a good public transport system, and trains run frequently to these stations from the main city-centre termini.

None of the walks in this collection are long or arduous, all being only two or three miles in length. I have deliberately not indicated how long each will take, since this depends entirely upon the walker and how much time they wish to spend looking at the sights on route. You do not need a map, although it is probably worth carrying a copy of the *Birmingham A to Z*.

Refreshments

Like all cities, Birmingham abounds with places to stop and get a drink or a meal, or buy a snack to take with you. All these walks will pass shops, cafés or pubs where you can buy refreshments. I have deliberately not recommended specific places, as these are too much a matter of personal taste.

Walk 1

Digbeth: the early beginnings of modern Birmingham

Until AD700 the site of modern Birmingham was largely ignored as an area to live. It was heavily forested, with soil too poor to make it worth farming, and the absence of major river valleys made communications difficult. There were many more attractive places for the small population of Britain to settle, but this altered in the seventh century when the mass arrival of Anglo-Saxons from the continent meant an increased pressure for land. These new settlers migrated from the fertile coastal plains, following river valleys into the heart of the country where they built small villages in clearings in the forest. The suffix 'ley' is Anglo-Saxon for 'clearing', and the earliest settlements such as Yardley, Beoley and Selly were on the more fertile land to the south of the modern conurbation. As the population expanded, secondary settlements grew up. Eventually, in around AD700, a local chieftain named Beorma (or 'Birm') led a tiny group of followers (or 'ingas') northwards to build a new hamlet (a 'ham'), and thus 'Birm-ingas-ham' came into existence.

This small hamlet was built on the southern side of a sandstone ridge (on top of which St Phillip's cathedral now stands), which provided shelter from the northern winds, between the ridge and the River Rea, at a place near where that river could be forded.

The land was just about adequate for farming, and for many years the settlers scraped out a meagre existence. By the time of the Domesday Book, 1086, there were less than a dozen poor families living in the manor of Birmingham, which was valued as being worth only £1 a year, one of the poorest manors in England. But Birmingham's future was not to lie in the soil, but in business, and within a couple of centuries Birmingham had expanded to become one of the biggest manors in Warwickshire, absorbing many of its richer neighbours. How did this transformation come about?

One family remained, with interruptions, lords of the manor of Birmingham for 500 years after 1086. They were entrepreneurs and, being unable to generate much wealth from farming, turned to trading instead. The ford through the River Rea provided a natural line of communication for cattle and trade goods moving through central England. By 1166 Birmingham had been granted the right to hold a regular weekly market, a lucrative industry since tolls could be imposed on traders and freedom from tolls given as a reward to people living in the area. Business, and with it settlement, increased, and in 1189 the status of 'town' was conferred. By 1330 Birmingham was the third largest town in Warwickshire and still growing. This expanding town was centred upon the original tiny Saxon hamlet founded by Beorma.

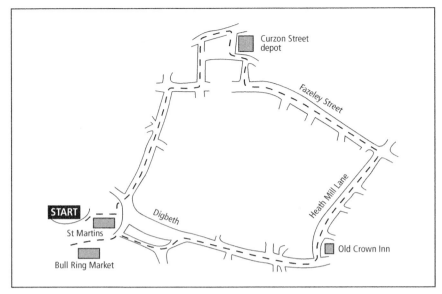

Start
The walk starts from the elevated concourse outside the Bull Ring Shopping Centre, looking down over St Martin's and the Bull Ring open-air market.

The original Saxon settlement, just a cluster of houses, was just below where you are now standing. The green sheds of the Birmingham Market occupy the ground where a fortified manor-house, the home of the Lords of Birmingham, stood. In front of the manor was an open area where the weekly market was held, and adjoining it was a flourishing cattle market. It is still a market place, with stalls now clustered around the silver tower in its centre. The original houses, little more than huts in many cases, were clustered around the manor and the market. A church (where the present St Martin's now stands) was a late

An open-air market has been held on the Bull Ring since Saxon days.

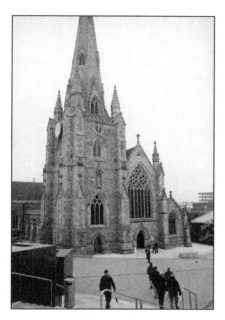

St Martin's, standing on the site of a Norman church.

addition to the village, probably first built in the late 1100s. If you walk to your left, to the far end of the concourse, you can see past St Martin's, down Digbeth. This is the line of the original mediaeval road that led down to the ford through the River Rea. The huge open fields where the villagers pursued their agriculture were between here and the river and beyond that would have been open forest and scattered villages. Behind you is the sandstone ridge that protected Birmingham from the worst of the weather.

Descend the steps to the front of St Martin's.

The first documentary evidence for a church on this site dates from 1263, although a church probably existed here since at least the middle of the 12th century. It was the only parish church for Birmingham until 1715. In the late Middle Ages the church had an aisled nave, a chancel, and a tower on its north-east side. The original church was built in grey-brown sandstone, and the interior was decorated with mediaeval wall paintings. In 1690 the outer walls were encased in brick, a brick-built clerestory was added in 1733 and a vestry in 1760. In 1855 the tower was restored and the spire built by Philip Charles Harwick, using the original sandstone, and then in 1872–75 the remainder of the church was demolished and carefully rebuilt by J.A. Chadwick. Chadwick also used original sandstone, matching Hardwick's restored tower, and made the church slightly larger than the mediaeval building, with transepts and chancel aisles added. The church was seriously damaged by a bomb in 1941, and repaired again in 1950–53. The interior of the church is sandstone, with an open timber roof and stained-glass windows by Edward Burne-Jones and William Morris (see Walk 10).

Walk ahead to the slender chrome spire in the centre of the Bull Ring open-air market.

Memorial to all who died during the Blitz.

This is the site of the mediaeval cattle market. Cattle were driven from Wales and from Leicestershire and brought here to market. The cattle market existed from the 12th century until 1769, when it was moved to Dale End as a 'temporary' measure. The site was cleared and became a general market in 1806 and has remained in use ever since, although today it is a shadow of its former self.

Just to your right is a memorial to those who died during the Blitz. Between October 1940 and April 1943 the German airforce made 365 raids on Birmingham, 77 of them involving heavy bombers. Central Birmingham was badly damaged, with over 9,000 civilian casualties, 2,241 of them fatal.

From the spire, walk with St Martin's on your left-hand side to reach the road, with the Bull Ring Tavern in front of you. Cross the road to reach the front of the Bull Ring Tavern and then turn right along Moat Lane.

Despite fanciful references to a 'Birmingham Castle', the home of the Lords of Birmingham was actually a fortified manor house, located behind where the multi-storey car park now stands. The original manor was a simple wooden structure, surrounded by a wooden palisade. As the family grew richer with the expansion of the town, the house was extended into a far more elaborate structure, the surrounding wall strengthened and a moat dug around its perimeter. Although the manor house had disappeared by the 16th century, its location, and that of its surrounding moat, is remembered in the street name.

Follow the road around to the left, with the Sing Fat Ltd Chinese Supermarket on the corner opposite, to reach Digbeth. Cross the road to the front of Digbeth Police Station and then turn right down Digbeth.

This road, descending gently into the valley of the River Rea, was the main artery of trade in and out of mediaeval Birmingham. Cattle were the original source of trade, and were driven into town up this road. By the Middle Ages

Birmingham, despite the fact that it had no mineral deposits within its boundaries, was already developing a strong manufacturing industry. Raw materials, such as iron, copper and precious metals, as well as fuel such as charcoal and later coal, were brought into the town, where skilled craftsmen manufactured metal goods. The process became self-fulfilling: the more Birmingham became a manufacturing centre, the more artisans and merchants were attracted into the town, further increasing its importance. Raw materials came into Birmingham, many from the north but also from the south, along this road, while manufactured goods went south along here to the markets of London and beyond. The tradition for manufacturing metal goods started in the early Middle Ages and continued, growing until by the mid-19th century Birmingham was the foremost manufacturing town in the world.

Follow the road to reach the traffic lights, with Birmingham College Information Centre opposite.

This is the location of the River Rea. Today it is channelled through underground culverts, but until the 18th century it flowed above ground. It was forded about where we stand now, and it was this ford that caused Beorma to locate his village where he did. Cattle were the original item of trade, driven up from Wales and Leicestershire, and then rested and washed here at the ford before being taken to Birmingham's cattle market for sale. Secondary industries related to cattle grew up around here. To your left, Milk Street was obviously a dairy market, while the area to your right, on the other side of Digbeth, became a centre for tanning and glue manufacture. The name of the nearby public house, the Big Bull's Head, is another reminder of the area's past.

Cross Milk Street to the front of Birmingham College. Keep ahead past the front of the college and cross the next road.

Although the Rea was never a major river, it was still wide enough to be a formidable barrier, especially in winter when rainwater caused it to flood its banks. It was not especially deep but could become very wide, and channels were built to control and divert its excess waters. Floodgate Street, which you are just crossing, follows the course of one of those channels.

Keep ahead along Digbeth Road.

On your right is Chapel House Street. Travel, certainly before the 15th century, was a hazardous undertaking, with rutted muddy roads going between isolated

The Old Crown Inn, dating from the 15th century.

towns and through dark forests. Small chapels were often built on the edges of towns, for wayfarers to pray in before and after journeys, and one such was built here, on the edge of town. The present Bull Ring trading estate stands on the site of the old chapel.

Follow Digbeth Road to traffic lights, with Heath Mill Lane on the left.

The town of Birmingham ended at the River Rea; half a mile ahead of you is Deritend, which in the Middle Ages was a separate community. Opposite you is the magnificent half-timbered Old Crown Inn, the only mediaeval building to survive in modern Birmingham's town centre. This was built in the late 15th century by the Guild of St John the Baptist of Deritend, one of the two guilds in Birmingham, religious orders to which only the town's richest citizens could belong. Such guilds flourished as a link between the church and secular society, and as well as spiritual support provided members with a form of social security and welfare benefit. This building was originally the Guildhall, where members of the guild met and prayed, and was also a school for the children of guild members. The Guildhall was timber-built, infilled with wattle and daub, and the original ground floor contains a large meeting hall and smaller master's room. The building was turned into an inn in the 19th century, and has recently been restored.

The Old Crown Inn can be visited during licensing hours.

St Basil's, built in 1910 in the Arts and Crafts style.

Turn left along Heath Mill Street, passing under the railway viaduct. Follow Heath Mill Lane to traffic lights, passing St Basil's on your right.

The Church of St Basil's was built in 1910–11, in the style known as Arts and Crafts Primitivism. Birmingham has a long association with the Arts and Crafts movement (see Walk 10) and this church was designed by A.S. Dixon, who was responsible for many buildings in the city. Today the church is a young person's training centre.

Turn left at the traffic lights.

Birmingham grew dramatically in the 19th century. Many new industrial concerns developed, heavy industry that built upon the manufacturing skills and traditional craftsmanship that had flourished in Birmingham for centuries. Although much of this heavy industry has now closed down again, it is still remembered in the names of buildings such as the Forge Mill Tavern opposite, built to accommodate workers in several nearby steel forges.

Walk along Fazeley Street.

On the right is the Bond, a development of luxury accommodation built inside a disused canal warehouse. The frontages of a row of 19th-century cottages have been incorporated into the development.

A little further on, also on the right, is an ex-canal basin. The canal was cut in 1796, linking the industries of Birmingham with markets across England (see Walk 6), and the L-shaped canal basin was added in 1840. Although the basin has been partly infilled and redeveloped, warehouses from its 19th-century heyday can still be seen.

Cross over Pickford Street and then over the canal.

The entrance to the former canal basin is visible to your right.

Just over the canal turn right into Andover Street. Follow Andover Street under a railway arch into Banbury Street. Turn right down Banbury Street to the gates of Gun Barrel Proof House.

One industry long associated with Birmingham is the manufacture of firearms, both side arms and artillery pieces. Demand increased dramatically during the

Early 19th-century Gun Barrel Proof House.

Curzon Street Depot.

Napoleonic Wars, when the Government turned to Birmingham to manufacture many of the guns needed by the army and navy. An Act of Parliament was passed in 1813 requiring an establishment be set up to prove (test) barrels and completed guns before they were sent on to the end-user. The Gun Barrel Proof House was built for that purpose, and it is still run by a Board of Guardians composed of master gun-makers.

Retrace your steps along Banbury Street and then take the first right into New Canal Street. Walk along to traffic lights.

On the right is the imposing Curzon Street Station. This was opened in 1838 as the terminus of the London & Birmingham Railway, the first mainline railway in Britain.

The western façade consists of massive Ionic columns, and the whole building is laced with blocks of ashlar. Inside, the entrance hall reaches all the way up to the roof, with a massive grand staircase sweeping up to the first floor. The building was the work of Philip Charles Chadwick, who also built St Martin's Church. Curzon Street Station was closed in 1854, after New Street Station was opened, and used for many years as goods offices. There are currently plans in place to develop it as a concert hall and headquarters for the Royal College of Organists.

Millennium Point.

Turn left at the traffic lights and walk along Curzon Street, railings around an open green area are on your left-hand side.

On your right is Millennium Point, built between 1997 and 2001 and now housing the Think Tank, the city's Museum of Science and Industry.

Turn left into Bartholomew Street. At the end of Bartholomew Street turn right and go up to the crossroads. Cross left over the road via the zebra crossing and turn left into Park Street.

Keep ahead, the Bull Ring Shopping Centre soon in sight ahead, and follow the road under a railway bridge to reach the broad and busy Moor Street Queensway. Cross the road at traffic lights to the front of the Selfridges building and keep ahead. Just before Street Martin's turn left up a ramp, leading back to steps on the right that take you back to the start.

Walk 2

Kings Norton: a walk through a mediaeval village

During the eighth century the pressure of an increasing population forced the Anglo-Saxons to expand northwards and eastwards, leaving the rich arable land of the Thames valley and the East Midlands and penetrating the heavily wooded area of the Forest of Arden. This forest was immense, spreading across much of the modern Midlands, and with its poorer soils and heavy tree cover it was not prime agricultural land. As we have seen, Mercian Saxons came from the east and founded a small settlement called Birmingham. To the south of them Saxons from the Hwicce confederation, originating from the Thames valley, founded small villages in the forest. This forested area south of the Birmingham plateau was part of the manor of Bromsgrove, a manor that was the property of the king, and in the most northerly part of that manor a village was built. That village became known as the king's north town, or 'Kings Norton'.

With the introduction of 'shires' by the Normans, Kings Norton became part of Worcestershire and remained so until the early 20th century. It was a small agricultural community until the 19th century and, even though the

The village green at Kings Norton.

development of railways and canals brought in its wake some measure of industry, Kings Norton remained a separate community, surrounded by green fields that separated it from the ever-growing sprawl of Birmingham. It was not until 1911 that, on recommendations from the Parliamentary Boundaries Commission, Kings Norton was incorporated into the City of Birmingham. Although today the conurbation has spread far to the south of Kings Norton, it still retains features of its mediaeval past and still has the feel of the separate community it once was.

Start

This walk starts from Kings Norton Station. There is a frequent train service between New Street Station and Kings Norton.

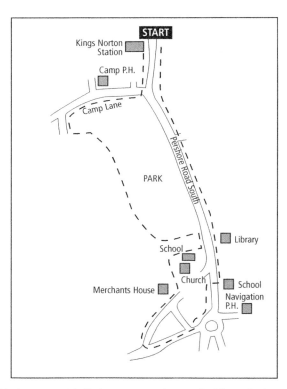

From the station, turn right down the main road (Pershore Road South). At the bottom of the hill turn right into Camp Lane. Follow Camp Lane past allotments on the left.

Allotments have always been an important feature of inner city life. In the late 19th and early 20th centuries most people lived in houses with little or no garden and, although the inhabitants of Kings Norton fared better than most of their counterparts in other parts of the city, few of them had sufficient land attached to their homes to grow more than the minimum of flowers or vegetables. From the early 20th century, councils in cities throughout Britain set aside plots of arable land that could be rented by their citizens, usually on an annual basis. The popularity of allotments reached its peak in the inter-war years, and although the number and acreage of allotments has declined substantially in the past three decades, there are still a considerable number to be found – islands of cultivation in the heart of Britain's cities.

Continue along Camp Lane, passing the Camp public house.

When England descended into civil war in 1642, King Charles sent his queen, Henrietta Maria, and his children to safety in Holland while he raised an army to fight against his own Parliament. Henrietta Maria was not pleased to be away from her husband: she had always been the stronger personality of the two, far more adamant regarding the preservation of royal privileges than the king, and she was worried that in her absence he would be swayed by advisers who favoured coming to a compromise with Parliament. In 1644 Henrietta Maria returned to England, landing at Bridlington in Yorkshire and, avoiding capture by Parliamentarian forces, soon joined with the Royalist general the Earl of Newcastle. The queen stayed with the northern army for some months, priding herself as a military commander and styling herself 'Generallissima'. Her aim, however, was always to be reunited with the king, currently at his wartime capital Oxford, and so, accompanied by a large troop of soldiers, she headed south. She avoided the Parliamentary forces sent to intercept her and soon arrived at Kings Norton.

Henrietta Maria herself lodged in the town. Her troops, some 3,000 foot soldiers, 30 companies of cavalry and 50 wagons, made camp here, just to the north of Kings Norton. The names of Camp Lane and the Camp public house commemorate that event.

Turn left into Eckershall Road. Cross a brook and keep along the road until opposite Wythall Lane. Turn left into a rose garden, signed 'Rea Valley Route'.

At the far right-hand corner of the rose garden take the tarmacked path across Kings Norton Park, with the spire of a church directly ahead.

Birmingham Corporation was formed in 1851, taking over the management of the city from the Street Commissioners. From its inception, the corporation was greatly concerned with improving the quality of life for Birmingham's ever-growing working class, as well as effectively managing the infrastructure of the rapidly expanding city. They recognised the need for public parks, green spaces open to all amid the urban sprawl that would provide 'the lungs of the city' for its citizens. This idea was revolutionary in mid-Victorian Britain, with hardly any of the country's expanding cities having gardens and open spaces to which access was free. Fortunately, Birmingham had a long tradition of Non-conformism and altruism, even among its richer citizens, and a number of the city's richer landowners donated land to the corporation for use as public parks and gardens. Birmingham's first park, Adderley Park, opened in 1856, Calthorpe Park opened the following year, and by the end of the century most boroughs had parks and open spaces where their inhabitants could, on their days off, relax in comparatively fresh air. Although the absorption of Kings Norton into Birmingham was strongly contested by the local population, one effect of its incorporation was that it gained numerous civic amenities, including a municipal park.

At a fork in the path take either route. Both lead to a second rose garden, where you should turn left to reach the road. Turn right along the road, passing a cemetery on your right. At the end of the cemetery, turn right up a drive.

The old half-timbered building on your left, currently under restoration after winning the 2004 BBC2 Restoration Competition, is the Old Grammar School. This tiny building was erected between 1434 and 1460, with the ground floor measuring only 30ft by 15ft, and with a similar sized first-floor room. The first floor is supported on stilts, giving rise

The Old Grammar School, built between 1434 and 1460.

to the theory that the ground floor may originally have been open. Its original purpose is unknown. It may have been a guildhall or more likely a chantry chapel. As there was no means of heating the building before the chimney and fireplace were installed in the 17th century, it is unlikely it was a residence.

There is record of a grammar school in Kings Heath from 1547 onwards, founded by Edward VI and with a schoolmaster paid a salary of £10 a year. Although it is not certain, it is most likely that the school was located in this building. In 1629 Thomas Hall was appointed master of the Kings Norton Grammar School and chaplain of the adjoining St Nicholas Church. Hall was a highly respected academic and a good teacher, with many of his pupils going on to study at Oxford University. Hall was also a devout Puritan, with strong views on theology and sociology, views on the place of women in society that bordered on the misogynistic, and political views that were strongly in support of the Parliamentarian cause in the growing conflict between king and Parliament. These views, especially once the Civil War had started in 1642, put Hall at odds with many of his congregation, Kings Norton being firmly Royalist. Hall survived the Civil War but was evicted from his position in 1662 when he refused to sign the Act of Uniformity. This Act restored the primacy of the Church of England and required all clergy to use its prayer book and also to swear allegiance to the newly-restored king, Charles II. Hall, along with a fifth of the clergy of England, would not agree to this Act, and lost his position.

The Grammar School continued to flourish. In the 18th century pupils, all boys, paid between 3d and 1s a week to attend and were taught Latin, French and mathematics. In the 19th century girls were admitted to the school and were taught separately in the upper room. The Grammar School was finally closed in 1878, when a new school was built just across the road.

Turn left to follow a tarmacked path to the church doors.

There may have been a church here in Saxon times, but the first recorded church dates from the late 11th century, when the Normans built a small chapel, only the size of the present chancel, dedicated to St Nicholas. The chapel was a subsidiary of its mother church in Bromsgrove, Kings Norton being part of the royal manor of Bromsgrove.

In 1231 King Henry III gave the manor to the Priory of Worcester, in exchange for which masses

St Nicholas's Church.

were to be said for his father, King John, and for himself after his death. The Priory set about extending its newly acquired property in Kings Norton: the chapel was rebuilt and enlarged, doubling its length to reach the line of the present north and south doorways, and adding the two aisles. The following century St Nicholas was further extended, with a new nave, aisles and chancel, and in the 15th century the porch was added as well as its crowing glory, the tower and spire. St Nicholas was still officially not a church but a 'chapel dependant', a subsidiary of Bromsgrove church, and it was not until 1846 that it became independent of its mother church and was established as the parish church of Kings Norton. In Victorian times the interior of the church was totally stripped of its fine mediaeval fittings and rebuilt, but the exterior largely escaped alteration.

Follow the path to a lychgate.

Facing you across the churchyard is a magnificent Merchant's House, a complex building added to over the centuries and known as the Saracen's Head. This building, like the Grammar School, is currently being restored after winning the BBC2 Restoration Competition.

The half-timbered North Range, facing the churchyard, is the oldest part of the building, erected in 1492 by a wealthy wool merchant. It was built to impress: there is a continuous 'jetty', or overhanging upper floor, along the

The North Range of the Merchant's House.

whole of the north side, and an impressive doorway, the original entrance to the building, leading in from the churchyard. The interior was equally grand, with a magnificent grand hall and a more intimate but equally imposing front parlour. It also had a brick chimney, a feature unusual in midland houses of that time, between the hall and parlour.

The original building was soon added to, with an extra two-storey half wing added in 1500 on to the north-eastern corner (the right as you look at it from the church), and a whole extra range added shortly afterwards on the eastern side, facing the green (the left as you look at it from the church).

In 1644 Queen Henrietta Maria stayed in this fine house while on her way south to join King Charles at Oxford. Her troops were camped on the other side of the church, on the area now covered by the park and Camp Lane. Most of the leading citizens of Kings Norton were staunchly Royalist, and the queen was welcomed and fêted during her stay. The Puritan Thomas Hall, curate of the church a mere 50 yards north of where Queen Henrietta Maria was staying, did not join in the celebrations. He was already in disgrace with many of his congregation for his pro-Parliament views, and his sermons were often boycotted.

The Eastern Range was originally half-timbered like the North Range, but this range was converted in the early 18th century into a small row of shops, faced with brick. At the end of the 18th century these shops were themselves knocked together to form an inn, the Saracens Head. A southern extension was added to the half-timbered building in the mid-16th century. This was demolished in the 18th century, and all trace of it eventually disappeared beneath the car park of the Bull's Head, although it is now being excavated and rebuilt as part of the restoration work.

Keep ahead on to the Green.

The village green was the centre of mediaeval villages, a place where the villagers could gather for festivities, for markets, and for any public meetings as occurred. The most important buildings in the village – the church, the inn if the village ran to one, often the manor house or the vicarage, were gathered around the green, with cottages behind them. This green has existed as long as the village of Kings Norton. Once it was much larger, but over the years housing and road widening has encroached upon it. There were regular markets held on the green and once a year since 1616 a 'Mop Fair' has been held. This was originally a hiring fair, held on the first Monday in October, where labourers would turn up and offer their services to the local farmers to get the harvest in. The Mop Fair is still held, and although now it is a fair in the modern sense of the word, a tradition going back nearly four centuries is upheld.

The line of the mediaeval roof can be seen on the modern Bulls Head.

Keep ahead, passing the Bull's Head on your right.

The Bull's Head was rebuilt in 1901, but an inn has stood on this spot facing on to the green for many centuries. The line of the original roof of the mediaeval inn can be seen on the side facing the car park.

Continue along the Green to the Post Office and Molly's Café, then turn left to continue around the Green.

No. 10 The Green is today the local Spar, but it is built into a much older building. If you look up to first-floor

The original half-timbered building above the shop frontage.

level you will see the original half-timbered building, dating from the 15th century. At one time all the buildings on the green would have been half-timbered.

Cross a zebra crossing in front of the pharmacy, then turn right down to the corner of the main road.

Just beyond the present traffic island is the site of the old cattle market, where cattle were brought on market days from many miles around for sale at the Kings Norton fair.

Further down the road opposite can be seen the Navigation Inn. This building dates from 1906 but replaced an earlier pub, opened on the banks of the Worcester & Birmingham Canal when it was cut in 1791. Although the canal was originally dug to connect industrial Birmingham and the potteries of Worcester, and beyond that eventually Bristol, it provided access to raw materials and markets as never before. Within a few decades industry reached the essentially rural community of Kings Norton, with a paper mill and a chemical works on the canal front.

Turn left along the main road to a light-controlled pedestrian crossing. Cross the road to the primary school.

Until the second half of the 19th century, education was a luxury available almost exclusively to the more affluent members of society. In 1838 only 20 per cent of children in Birmingham received any type of formal education. By 1868 that number had doubled to 40 per cent, but even then the average length of time a child spent at school was only two years. Much of the schooling took place in charity schools, of greater or lesser quality, and attendance was voluntary. The Birmingham Education Society, founded by George Dixon and supported by leading citizens like Joseph Chamberlain, joined with other national organisations in campaigning for formal, state-funded education. The 1870 Education Act was a half-hearted measure that left most schools under the control of religious organisations and still required a payment of 3d a week for pupils, a modest sum that was nonetheless beyond the reach of many working-class people.

The Birmingham School Board, founded under the provisions of the 1870 Act, was a pioneering body that blazed a trail for the rest of the country to follow. It initially reduced the weekly fee and then in 1891 abolished it altogether. It widened the school curriculum to include science and also practical courses such as woodwork and cookery, it provided kindergarten

Kings Norton school, opened in 1902.

teaching on a limited scale and it improved the physical buildings of schools and added tarmacked playgrounds. By the time the 1902 Education Act abolished all school boards and transferred their powers to local authorities, Birmingham offered a standard of education that was little bettered anywhere in England.

The Kings Norton Primary School was established in 1878, replacing the old grammar school. Initially classes were for both sexes, but separate entrances for boys and girls were retained. A large tarmacked playground surrounded the school and the classrooms were large, airy and well lit. The school was extended in 1902 and retains many of the features of that era.

Turn left along the main road.

No. 288 Pershore Road, which now incorporates a nursery, was built as the house for the schoolmaster. Not only did

Separate entrances for boys and girls.

the Birmingham School Board provide good facilities for pupils, but it also aimed to attract and retain high-calibre teachers. Dedicated accommodation for the headmasters was not uncommon.

Continue along the road, passing the library.

Prior to 1850, it was necessary to pay to go into libraries or museums, and thus access was confined to the more affluent classes. In that year Parliament passed the Free Libraries and Museums Act, which gave councils the power to add a halfpenny to the rates, in order to provide cultural and intellectual stimulation to the working masses who could not otherwise afford access to their own heritage. Unfortunately, the Act required a two-thirds majority of voters (and at that time the franchise was still limited to middle-class property owners) to support any such measures, and when the newly formed Birmingham Corporation introduced a proposal in 1852 to raise the rates to pay for free libraries, it was defeated. It was not until 1861 that Birmingham's first free library was opened, on Constitution Hill, and it was so popular that potential users queued for over an hour to obtain their library ticket. Emboldened by this success, the council made a modest extension to the library service in 1868, providing for one library to service each of the four quarters of the city, together with a central reference and lending library. This still did not satisfy the public appetite for books, and over the next three decades publicly-funded free libraries were opened throughout the city and also in the communities adjoining the city boundaries. This library was a comparatively late arrival, being opened in 1905 to serve the growing population of Kings Norton.

Follow the main road, crossing a brook, to traffic lights.

This brook is the River Rea, the main water supply for Kings Norton until the late 18th century. There were a number of mills along the river, dating from the Middle Ages, used for grinding local corn. Despite the cutting of the canal in 1791, Kings Norton remained a quiet rural community until well into the 19th century, separated from Birmingham by green fields.

Cross Melchett Road and keep ahead up the hill. At the top of the hill cross the road to the station.

Walk 3

Aston Hall: the story of Birmingham's stateliest home

At the time of the Domesday Book, the manor of Birmingham was small and impoverished, home to a dozen families and worth only £1 a year. It was dwarfed, both in wealth and population, by the manors around it. Handsworth was worth £5 a year, Yardley £8, but the richest manor of all was Aston. There was little in the way of a village in Aston manor, but unlike Birmingham it had rich farmland, valuable woodland, and a corn mill on the River Tame. It was home to at least 40 families, living mostly in scattered farms and cottages, and had its own church with a shared priest. After the Norman Conquest Aston was given to William FitzAnsculf, a soldier of fortune who had helped William the Conqueror to the throne, a rich reward indeed compared to the gift of the manor of Birmingham to a Lord Peter, surname unknown.

FitzAnsculf built a manor house just to the north of the parish church of Aston, on swampy ground near the River Tame, but this was soon abandoned in favour of a more suitable site in Duddeston. FitzAnsculf and his descendants did little to develop Aston, being content to live on the wealth its rich farming land generated. In the early 14th century the manor of Aston passed to the Holte family, who concentrated their energies on acquiring wealth through land. But by then Birmingham had developed into the third-largest town in

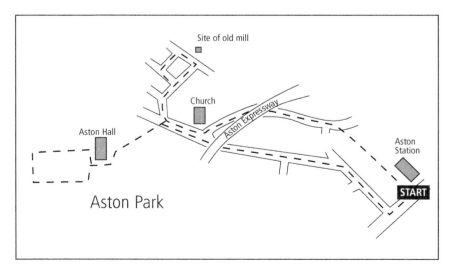

St Peter & St Paul Church, Aston.

Warwickshire and was the centre of trade and industry for the area, and the days of Aston's pre-eminence were over.

Start
This walk starts from Aston railway station. There is a frequent service from Birmingham New Street to Aston.

From Aston Station turn right and then immediately turn right again up a pathway between the station and the Methodist Church. At the end of the pathway turn left along Aston Hall Road. Cross over the road and follow the road under the elevated Aston Expressway, then turn right into the churchyard and follow the path to the church door.

This is the parish church of St Peter & St Paul. Under the Saxons and the Normans the manor of Aston had been large but diffuse. There was never one large village central to the manor, but instead there were numerous small hamlets scattered over a large area. Although this was the parish church of the manor of Aston, it was not local to most of the manor's tenants, and daughter chapels were built in Deritend, Castle Bromwich, Ward End and Water Orton to serve the needs of its scattered parishioners. Today's church, although it stands on the site of the early Saxon and Norman churches, has undergone drastic expansion and reconstruction over the centuries. The church we see now is largely Victorian.

Leave the churchyard and bear left back to the main road. Cross the road at the zebra crossing, turn right and then bear left into Aston Park.

By the 1530s the Holte family, owners of the manor of Aston, were renting some of their land in the south of the manor to the rising industrialists of Birmingham. Thomas Holte, an eminent lawyer, was employed by Thomas

Aston Hall.

Cromwell in the process known to history as the Dissolution of the Monasteries. As Cromwell's agent, Holte was well placed to profit from the sale of religious property, and the family wealth increased dramatically. The fortunes of the Holte family flourished under the Tudors. Thomas's son Edward became Sheriff of Warwickshire. Edward's son, named Thomas after his eminent grandfather, went further. Not only did he succeed his father as Sheriff in 1598, but in 1603 he was part of the deputation that offered the Crown of England to King James of Scotland upon the death of Queen Elizabeth. For this he was rewarded with a knighthood. Sir Thomas, as he was then called, continued to loyally support King James, donating large sums of money to finance the king's war in Ireland, for which he was rewarded with the title of Baronet in 1612.

The Holte family seat was still Duddeston Hall, two miles south of modern Aston and built in the 12th century by the FitzAnsculf lords of the manor. But in 1618 Thomas Holte decided to build a new home, more in keeping with his new status. Taking advantage of the Enclosures Act, Sir Thomas enclosed the common land around Aston itself, removing rights of farming and grazing his tenants had enjoyed for centuries and creating a huge private park. Within this park Sir Thomas built Aston Hall.

Keep ahead to Aston Hall.

Aston Hall was attacked by Parliamentary militia during the Civil War.

Work began on Aston Hall in 1618. By 1631 enough was built for Sir Thomas to move into his new home, but the hall was not finally finished until 1635. Some £60,000 had been spent on its construction, a huge amount by the standards of the day.

The hall was designed by architect John Thorpe. It is one of the last Jacobean buildings in England, and one of the greatest. It is built in the shape of a half H, with a central range containing the main hall and with a projecting entrance lobby, flanked by two projecting wings. The wings and the central range are capped by domed towers, there are curved gables to the roof line and splendid chimneys that hark back to the great Elizabethan country houses. In front of the hall are two courtyards, with lodges to either side connected to the main building by low walls.

In October 1642 King Charles stayed for two nights at Aston Hall, while inspecting the troops raised locally to fight on his behalf in the imminent Civil War. Sir Thomas was staunchly Royalist, while Aston, along with most of Birmingham, was equally staunchly Parliamentarian. In 1643 a largely untrained band of Parliamentary militia, 1,200 strong, attacked and captured Aston Hall, killing 12 of the soldiers Sir Thomas had left there as a garrison and capturing the rest.

Turn left along the front of the hall, and walk around the hall to view the formal gardens at the rear of the building. Go through the gardens and down the steps at the rear.

Formal gardens to the rear of Aston Hall.

Sir Thomas Holte died in 1654 and was succeeded as 2nd Baron Holte by his grandson Robert. Aston Hall remained in the Holte family until 1782, when Charles, 6th Baron Holte, died. The hall passed to Sir Charles's daughter Mary and through her to her husband, Abraham Bracebridge of Atherstone. After 1794 the hall was leased out to various tenants, and in 1818 it was rented by James Watt, son of Birmingham's famous engineer and industrialist. Watt restored the hall, now fallen somewhat into decay, and improved the gardens.

Turn left along the path through the park.

James Watt died in 1848 and two years later Aston Hall and the 170 remaining acres of parkland that surrounded it were offered to the newly formed Birmingham Corporation for £150,000. The corporation was not interested in spending public money in this way, and it looked as if the hall and park would follow the rest of the estate and be used for housing. A 'Save Aston Hall' campaign was launched in 1856, resulting in the formation of a company which two years later acquired the hall and 43 acres of surrounding parkland to save it for posterity. However, only £9,000 of the £35,000 asking price had been raised, and for the next six years the company struggled to raise the remaining money. It was not until 1864, after the personal intervention of Queen Victoria, that Birmingham Corporation agreed to buy the hall and park for public use.

Birmingham Corporation added an additional six acres to Aston Park in 1873. As Aston became increasingly populated, with many working-class inhabitants living in small and overcrowded houses, the park became an important recreational facility. The hall was refurbished in the late 19th century. It was used as an art gallery until the opening of the new city-centre art gallery in 1885, and continued to be used to exhibit natural history collections, antiquities and works of art.

Turn left back to the front of the hall, and then go down the main driveway to the road.

During World War Two public air-raid shelters were built in the park, in the grounds to the right of the main drive you are now walking down.

Cross the road by the zebra crossing and turn left. Turn right into Holte Road. Keep right into Serpentine Road and follow it to its end.

The last of the Holtes, Dame Sarah, widow of the 5th Baron, died at Aston Hall in 1794. After her death the hall was rented out, and much of the park and surrounding land was sold to the banking firm of Greenway, Greaves & Whitehead.

Air-raid shelters were dug in Aston Park during World War Two.

In 1820 they started to lease out plots of land for building, and in the 1830s an area of expensive middle-class houses known as New Town was developing.

Throughout the 19th century the demand for cheap housing from Birmingham's ever-growing working class continued to grow. The city went on growing inexorably, spreading from the south to the hill-top where Aston Hall stood. New Town expanded, with ever-growing numbers of cheaper, smaller houses being crammed on to every available plot of land, altering the nature of the area and causing the original middle-class occupants to move out. In 1911 Aston was formally incorporated into the city of Birmingham.

Turn left along Village Road.

Behind the houses on the right-hand side of the road is the River Tame. In the Middle Ages there was a corn mill on the river at this spot, serving the hall and the hamlet of Aston.

Turn left along Charles Street and at its end turn left again into Yew Tree Road. At its end turn right back into Serpentine Road, then bear right along Holte Road back to the church. Keep ahead to cross traffic lights, and then continue ahead under the Aston Expressway. Keep ahead along Queens Road, past factories and a police station on your left. At a T-junction turn right into Grosvenor Road. Follow this road to traffic lights, at which point turn left. Aston Station is a few yards along on the left.

Walk 4

Sarehole Mill: a story of millers and Middle Earth

In the Middle Ages, owning a mill was a highly lucrative enterprise. Villagers were required by their feudal landlord to have their corn ground into flour at the local mill, for which the miller charged a fee. Prices for milling were frequently fixed by the landlord, who took a percentage of the miller's takings, the prices for which were on top of any rent he charged. To cover this the miller often increased the prices he charged and so was often seen as greedy and money-grasping, and deeply disliked by his own community.

In flat or exposed countryside, mills were wind-powered. Where there was a ready number of fast-running streams, water power was favoured. The rivers flowing south from the Birmingham plateau were ideal for water mills, and there were once over 70 watermills within the boundaries of modern Birmingham, 13 along the River Cole alone. Today only two survive. Sarehole Mill was built later than most of Birmingham's water mills, in a small hamlet in the countryside south of Birmingham. It was not confined to milling flour but shared in the towns burgeoning industrialisation.

Sarehole and its mill have a second claim to fame. For four of the most formative years of his life, the author J.R.R. Tolkien lived in Sarehole, and its people, its mill and its surrounding fields and woods were to be the model for the Shire in *The Lord of the Rings*.

Sarehole Mill has stood since the 16th century.

Start

This walk starts from Yardley Wood Station. There are frequent trains from Moor Street Station.

From the station proceed out on to the main road. Turn right for a few yards and cross the road at traffic lights. Turn left and follow the road downhill, past shops, a café and the Behan Arms pub.

Cross a side road and keep ahead through a squeeze stile, just to the side of imposing wrought-iron gates. Keep ahead into a green open space.

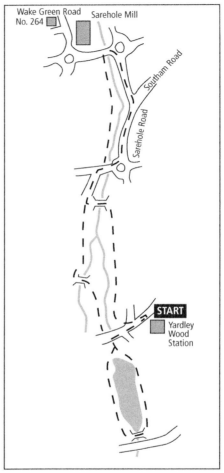

This area is known as the Dingles. In Saxon times it was part of the field system that surrounded the village of Yardley (the suffix 'ley' is Anglo-Saxon for a clearing in a forest, and Yardley originated as a small hamlet in an area cleared from the surrounding Forest of Arden). Around all villages in the Middle Ages were two or three huge fields, in which each villager would have the right to cultivate strips of land. The length of each strip was dictated by the lie of the land, but the width was always approximately 16.5ft, the width a team of oxen could conveniently plough. As the plough moved along the strip, it threw up earth into a bank, which became the boundary between the strips. When the light is right, particularly early on a summer's evening, the faint outlines of these mediaeval strips can still be seen here in the Dingles.

On reaching the banks of a stream turn right. Follow the green sward along the stream bank. Where the sward narrows, ignore a parapet-less bridge on the left but keep ahead on a narrow path, the river still on your left.

At the end of the path turn left over a brick-parapetted bridge. Go through a gate and turn right along a quiet cul-de-sac to reach a main road. Cross the road and turn right over a road bridge to a roundabout.

Turn left into Sarehole Lane. Follow the road as it curves left.

On the right is Southam Road, boyhood home to the comedian Tony Hancock. Although Sarehole Lane is a busier thoroughfare these days, the area still has a certain quiet gentility, and in the 1930s, when Hancock was a youth, it would have epitomised the middle-class suburbia the comic so often satirised in his work.

At a roundabout turn left to reach pedestrian-controlled lights. Cross the road to reach Sarehole Mill.

The first mill was built at Sarehole in 1542, when the lord of Yardley manor, Daniel Benford, gave permission for John Bedell to erect a corn mill. By that time feudalism was over, and Bedell's was a purely cash venture. Unlike in earlier times, the local population had no legal obligation to use his mill. Nevertheless Bedell was still in a monopoly position with the local farmers, who needed their corn ground, and the mill flourished. Biddles (or Bedells) mill was water driven, the power to drive the millstones being generated by a large watermill powered by the flow of the River Cole. Over the two centuries the mill passed through many hands, and en route diversified away from simply grinding corn. By a nice piece of lateral thinking, it had long been realised that the waterwheel generated power for as long as the river flowed, more power than the millstones alone needed, and so the extra power was diverted into water-powered machinery for grinding knives and rolling metal. In 1721 the mill, now known as High Wheels Mill, was bought by the Eaves family, who let it to various tenants. These included, from 1756 to 1761, the great industrialist Matthew Boulton, who used the mill to produce sheet metal for his factory in Snow Hill. In 1761 Boulton built a new factory in Handsworth which could manufacture its own sheet metal, and transferred his production there.

The next tenant, John Jones, continued the tradition of sharpening cutlery and edged tools at the mill as well as grinding corn. In 1775 Richard Eaves, the mill's landlord, went bankrupt, and Sarehole Mill, now used purely for milling corn again, was sold. In 1800 the mill was owned by William Deakin and his sons, who specialised in producing blades and gun-barrels for the East India Company. Deakin installed a second millwheel in 1807, increasing the mill's capacity. It continued to be used throughout the 19th century, always grinding

Nineteenth-century renovations to the mill.

corn but also being used for other purposes such as wire drawing and grinding animal bones for use as fertiliser. Sarehole Mill was an important source of flour during World War One, when demand was high, but like many other watermills it fell into disuse after the end of the war, unable to compete with industrial scale mills powered by coal. The mill was restored in 1969 and opened to the public under the care of Birmingham Museums & Art Gallery.

Sarehole Mill is open 11.30am–4pm, Tuesday–Sunday, admission free.

To see the house where the young J.R.R. Tolkien lived, turn right out of the gates to Sarehole Mill and walk to the roundabout. Turn right here along Wake Green Road for 200 yards. The half-timbered building on the left, No. 264, was Tolkien's childhood home, and is today a private residence.

John Ronald Reuel Tolkien was born in 1892 in South Africa, where his father Arthur had moved to from his Birmingham home to take a post as a bank manager. In 1895 Tolkien's mother Mabel returned to England to visit her parents in Kings Heath, bringing John and his brother Hilary. Arthur intended to join them the following year, but died unexpectedly. Mabel decided to stay in England and rented a cottage in Sarehole, Gracewell Cottage in Wake Green Road, where she and the boys lived for the next four years.

No.264 Wake Green Road, childhood home of J.R.R. Tolkien.

Trittiford Pond, the millpond
for Sarehole Mill.

These were idyllic years for the young Tolkien. In those days Sarehole was a tiny hamlet, just a collection of small cottages and scattered houses clustered around the mill, surrounded by fields, woods and streams, and with only narrow unmade country lanes connecting Sarehole with the outside world. Although the urban sprawl of Birmingham was only a couple of miles up the road, it felt a million miles away to a small boy for whom Sarehole felt like it was in the middle of the countryside. With his brother Tolkien spent his free time exploring the area around his home, and its rural tranquillity became the inspiration for the Shire in *The Hobbit* and especially *The Lord of the Rings*. The boys often played in Sarehole Mill, and were frequently chased away by the flour-coated miller's son, whom they christened 'the white ogre'. Sarehole Mill later re-emerged in Tolkien's books as Ted Sandyman's Mill.

Tolkien gained a place at King Edwards Grammar School in Kings Heath in 1900, and shortly afterwards moved away from Sarehole. Although he went on to study at the Hagley Road Oratory (see Walk 9) and later at Oxford, Sarehole remained with him as a memory of an idealised rural existence, which he later immortalised in his books. By the 1930s the fields of Sarehole had disappeared, built over by the encroaching suburbia of Birmingham, much to Tolkien's dismay when he returned for a visit after the war. His emotions at this ending of a rural idyll inspired the 'Scouring of the Shire' chapter at the end of *The Lord of the Rings*.

To continue the walk, leave the mill and cross the road at the traffic lights. Bear left and go through a gate beside a stile. Follow the tarmacked path through the woods.

On your left is the River Cole, used to power Sarehole Mill. The tree-lined stream winding through woods still carries echoes of the rural playground of the young Tolkien.

On reaching a road cross over and keep ahead along Coleside Avenue opposite. At the end of the cul-de-sac keep ahead across the visitors' car park, then keep ahead through a kissing gate beside a green metal gate. Keep ahead along a gravelled path. Ignore a bridge on your left but keep straight on along the path, through trees.

Keep straight on along a grassy sward, the stream still on your left, to soon reach a footbridge on your left. Cross the bridge and turn right, water now on both sides of you.

The water supply from the meandering River Cole was not reliable enough to keep Sarehole Mill running all year round. In 1768 Richard Eaves got permission from John Taylor, lord of the manor of Yardley, to construct a 'head race'. This was an artificial channel, straightened to allow water to flow faster, which took water from a mill pool upstream directly to the mill. It followed the course of the River Cole, thus doubling the water supply and also speeding up the flow. As you walk along, the unchannelled River Cole is to your left, while the artificial head race is to your right.

Follow the woodland path, with water on both sides, to reach a gate on to a road, a traffic island off to your right. Cross the road, bear right along the pavement for a few yards, then go left through a squeeze gate on to a green open sward. Keep ahead to reach the lake.

This lake is Trittiford Mill Pool, artificially created by John Eaves in 1861 to act as a reservoir for water flowing along the River Cole. The water was collected here and released as required via sluice gates into either the River Cole or the head race, or both.

Walk around the lake, the water on your left-hand side. At the end of the lake, turn left over a footbridge, but before you do, go out on to the lane ahead and turn left for a few yards to see the ford.

Ford through the River Cole.

Trittiford Ford has been used since Saxon times for the road from Yardley to cross the River Cole. With its tree-lined banks and tranquil waters, it seems incongruous to see such a ford still existing within the boundaries of the city of Birmingham.

Once across the footbridge turn left to follow the path around the pool. At the end of the pool keep ahead across the grass to the squeeze gate you entered by.

Turn right and follow the road across a bridge. Keep ahead up the road to return to Yardley Wood Station.

Walk 5

Religion and Retailing in Birmingham: a walk from the Bull Ring to St Chad's

From 1500 onwards Birmingham grew rapidly. In that year the population was only a few thousand, but by 1800 it was 74,000. Birmingham had established a reputation as a vibrant manufacturing centre, with skilled workmanship and a flourishing market. Unlike many older and more established towns, it was not dominated by mediaeval trades guilds, and so its entrepreneurial spirit was not restricted by strong regulation. As well as manufacturing and exporting goods, there has always been a strong retailing presence in Birmingham, selling to outsiders as well as to the town's own population.

Also, Birmingham has always played host to a wide variety of religions and beliefs. Skilled craftsmen moved into Birmingham, enticed by the free working environment, and many of them were political or religious Non-conformists, attracted to the more liberal atmosphere in the city. Many Irish moved into

Birmingham, bringing with them their own religion, Catholicism. Other religious dissenters also entered, for as a newer town Birmingham was less dominated by the organised church than elsewhere.

Start

The walk starts at the Nelson Statue, on the raised concourse outside the Bull Ring Shopping Centre, overlooking St Martin's.

Look down from the concourse to St Martin's Church.

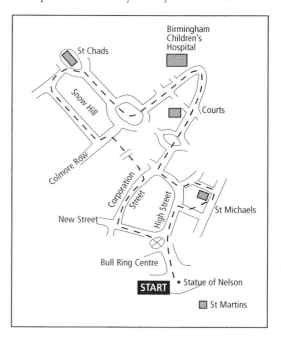

47

St Martin's-in-the-Bullring.

The first documentary evidence for a church on this site is 1263, although a church probably existed here from at least the middle of the 12th century. It was the only parish church for Birmingham until 1715. By the late 17th century the population had increased so much that St Martin's was extremely overcrowded, both the church itself and the adjoining graveyard, the only Anglican cemetery in the town. St Martin's was lost in a sea of shops and market stalls. The town had also spread geographically, up on to the ridge to the north. The solution was the building of an additional church, St Phillip's, opened in 1715 (see Walk 10).

The church as you see it today is the result of careful restoration in Victorian times, which returned St Martin's to much the appearance it had in the Middle Ages. The reconstruction of the Bull Ring in 1997 has opened up the area around the church, making St Martin's the dramatic centrepiece of the scene once again.

Now look over the open market, beside St Martin's Church.

From the foundation of Birmingham in the 10th century this open area, flanked by the church and the manor house (where the sheds of Birmingham Market now stand), was the heart of the town. The cattle market was here, and from 1166 a weekly general market took place. Semi-permanent stalls and shops grew up around the market. In 1769 the cattle market was moved to Dale End, leaving an open market square, crowded with stalls. To the north of the square, where you are now standing, was a row of butchers' stalls, known as the Shambles, and an arc of mostly wooden buildings, rising up the steep slope behind you to the High Street. A huge indoor market, the Market Hall, stood at the top of the slope.

During World War Two Birmingham was heavily bombed. Between October 1940 and April 1941 there were 77 raids by German heavy bombers, causing great loss of life and property throughout the city. The last and heaviest raid was on the night of 9–10 April 1941, when much of the area around the Bull Ring, including the Market Hall and many of the surrounding shops, was devastated. This destruction did, however, provide the opportunity to rebuild the city's shopping centre in a revolutionary way. The result was the Bull Ring Centre, the first shopping mall in Britain, which stood where you are now. Completed in 1967, it was a large block of indoor squares and markets on several levels, surrounded by elevated roads and pedestrian walkways. Although with hindsight it can be seen that many mistakes were made in its design, leading to the centre being decried as a piece of 'sixties brutalism', which subjugated the needs of shoppers and pedestrians to those of traffic and business, it was revolutionary in its conception and paved the way for future shopping centres across the country.

Tiers of old stalls climbed the slope where the modern Bull Ring now stands.

Horatio Nelson.

In 1997 a plan was approved to demolish the old Bull Ring Centre and rebuild it along modern lines that avoided the mistakes of the past. Central to that plan was the construction of the open concourse on which you are standing, with its feeling of space and its views over the original Bull Ring.

Turn around and look at the statue of Horatio Nelson behind you.

At the Battle of Trafalgar in 1805 Admiral Horatio Nelson inflicted a crushing defeat upon the combined navies of France and Spain and saved Britain from the threat of imminent invasion. Nelson died at the moment of his great victory, and almost immediately Britain was gripped by a wave of 'Nelson-mania'. The dead hero was idolised across the country and many statues were erected in his honour. The first such statue was here in Birmingham, despite the fact that 19th-century Birmingham had few statues in its centre compared to other cities, and had no connection with the sea. This statue was sculpted by Sir Richard Westmacott between 1807 and 1809, and then cast in bronze. It was paid for by many small donations, totalling over £2,000, raised by ordinary citizens of Birmingham. The statue originally stood in the centre of the old Bull Ring, in front of St Martin's. It was removed for protection during the Blitz and finally restored to its present position in 2003.

2002 statue of a bull, guarding the entrance to the Bull Ring shopping centre.

The Rotunda, icon of 1960s Birmingham.

With your back to the statue, walk up the broad pedestrianised walkway, with shops to both sides, to reach the Rotunda.

This open pedestrianised walkway, flanked by the huge glass windows of retail outlets, is central to the conception of the new Bull Ring Centre, which was opened in 2003. The claustrophobic feel of the old centre, where all the walkways were indoors, has been replaced by a much lighter and airier structure, with much of the access possible from the open air. The larger-than-life statue of a bull, sculpted by Laurence Broderick in 2002, guards the main entrance and maintains a link with a thousand-year past.

The Rotunda is a 24-storey concrete tower, standing 271ft high, which was built in 1964–65 as the centrepiece of the Bull Ring Shopping Centre. The tower is supported both by columns around the perimeter and a central core sunk on to foundation piles. At this, the podium level, there are shops and a double-height banking hall, and the floors above house offices. The mosaic cladding panels are not curved, but join at angles, giving the tower its iconic shape. The Rotunda was so much a symbol of post-war Birmingham that it was the only part of the old Bull Ring Centre to be retained when the rest was demolished.

Keep ahead past the Rotunda to a junction of streets, then bear right into High Street.

The High Street, running north from the Bull Ring, is the oldest street in the city. The original settlement in Birmingham was clustered at the foot of the slope, around the Bull Ring. During the Middle Ages the town steadily grew in size, both down towards the River Rea and up the slope (now occupied by the Bull Ring). By the 16th century Birmingham was growing out along the southern edge of the sandstone ridge upon which we are now standing. The High Street was laid down at that time, lined with timber-framed buildings that survived until the 19th century. Today all the buildings are 20th century, but the line of the road is still the same as it was 500 years earlier.

At the end of the pedestrianised street, just past Marks & Spencers, turn right down Carrs Lane.

On the left-hand side of the road, nestling between modern stores, is a wonderful survival of Birmingham's past, namely the shop of W.M. Powell & Son, Gun & Rifle Makers. Nineteenth-century Birmingham was one of the foremost manufacturers of guns in the world, both artillery and small arms, and much of this manufacturing was done by skilled craftsmen working in small family businesses (see also Walk 1). The building dates from 1860–61, but the company was founded half a century earlier and started manufacturing rifles for the British Army during the Napoleonic Wars.

Bear left across a small green garden.

The Carrs Lane United Reform (or Unitarian) chapel was founded in 1748, although the building has been rebuilt several times since then. Birmingham expanded dramatically as a manufacturing town in the 15th and 16th centuries. As a newer town, Birmingham was less dominated than elsewhere by those twin pillars of mediaeval conformity, the trades guilds and the church. The more entrepreneurial craftsmen often tended to be both religious Non-conformists and independent of any guild. Baptists, Methodists, and Quakers all came to the city, often settling in specific districts. The Unitarians, religious Non-conformists, were strongly established in this part of Birmingham by the mid-18th century.

Go right down the side of the Unitarian Reformed Church to reach Moor Street Queensway. Turn left along Moor Street Queensway for 30 yards and then turn left into Dingleys Passage.

On your left is St Michael's, a church built near the site of an 18th-century Unitarian chapel called the new Meeting House, which in turn had been built to replace an earlier Old Meeting House just across Moor Street. Although 18th-century Birmingham was home to a considerable mixture of different religious groups, things were not always harmonious. Religious freedom of thought often went hand-in-hand with political dissention. Non-conformists were often resented and their motives feared by those of orthodox religious and political persuasion. When Charles Wesley, the founder of Methodism, preached in 1764 at the newly opened chapel here in Moor Street, his sermon was disrupted by protest riots. There were anti-Catholic riots in 1780 and attacks on Quaker meeting houses in 1782.

Trouble really came to a head in 1791. The ideals of the French Revolution – liberty, equality and fraternity – were very attractive to some Liberals and Radicals, who were often religious dissenters as well. Joseph Priestley was a Unitarian minister whose chapel stood here on the site of St Michael's and who used his pulpit to praise the revolutionaries in France. His views were both provocative and alarming to many of Birmingham's more conservative citizens. On 6 July 1791 a meeting was hosted by Priestley at the Dadley Hotel in Temple Row to celebrate the anniversary of the storming of the Bastille. The hotel was attacked by anti-French/anti-liberal protesters who, increasingly drink-inflamed, then marched here, where they smashed up the New Meeting House. They then crossed Moor Street to burn the Old Meeting House to the ground, before spreading out into the suburbs to attack the houses of leading dissenters (see Walk 9).

Only 12 rioters were arrested in the aftermath of the 'Priestley Riots', and only two were ultimately convicted. Public opinion, while asserting the importance of law and order, nevertheless took the view that the victims had brought trouble on their own heads through their radical views.

Follow the road, with the multi-storey car park on your right-hand side, up to traffic lights, with Lloyds TSB on the left corner. Cross the road at the lights and then turn left for 30 yards to reach a junction of roads. Turn right up Bull Street.

DO NOT go down the subway but keep up the road to a crossroads and there turn right into Corporation Street. Cross over to the left-hand side of the road.

Follow Corporation Street to a main road and keep ahead across an open area with shrubs and seats.

This area, the open space and enclosing road, is Old Square, now a traffic island but once the most fashionable and exclusive part of Birmingham.

In the 13th century Birmingham was still only a very small town, with a population of less than 1,000, all clustered around the manor house, the church and the market square. Here, on what was then open land above the town, a small Priory was built, the Hospital of St Thomas of Canterbury. It was founded to provide accommodation for pilgrims en route to nearby Lichfield Cathedral and was intended to sustain itself by agriculture. It was not very efficient and made little impression on the region, although it is still remembered in the name of the main road leading north and south from this square, Priory Queensway.

After the Dissolution of the Monasteries, the Priory and its land were initially acquired by the Holte family of Aston (see Walk 3), then passed to the Smallbrookes and eventually to John Pemberton in 1687. By then Birmingham was expanding rapidly, its population now 15,000. Most still lived in small houses or tenements, crowded around the market square, but the more affluent of the townsfolk were moving up on to the ridge. Pemberton employed a local architect, Thomas Kempsey, to create the town's first planned development. This consisted of four primary streets of two-storey brick houses radiating out from a central square, called Old Square, in the middle of which was a tree-lined grassy area surrounded by iron railings. The square itself was lined with three-storey town houses, with railings in front to keep passers-by at bay. Pemberton himself lived on the square and the other houses were sold leasehold to prominent businessmen and professionals. To maintain the exclusivity of the area, known as the Priory Estate, leaseholders had to agree not to keep pigs, dump muck or run businesses from their homes.

The Priory Estate was the first stage of the gentrification of Birmingham. As the town expanded, better class housing spread out from Old Square, mainly towards the new St Phillip's Cathedral, but for a century Old Square was the most prestigious address in Birmingham. The nature of the area changed in the 19th century, as the more affluent citizens moved out to the suburbs and the properties were increasingly given over to business use. The last of Pemberton's fine old houses was still standing at the start of the 20th century, but was finally swept away in reconstruction during the 1960s. The central square was paved in 1998.

Keep ahead towards Tesco on the corner, and continue along Corporation Street.

The row of buildings on the right-hand side is the finest surviving example of the magnificent town houses built in 1885–86 as part of the last redevelopment of this area for residential use. Today the buildings are offices. Also on the right

The Victoria Law Courts, built in 1887–91.

is the Methodist Central Hall. John Wesley had preached in Birmingham in 1764, and the city's first dedicated Wesleyan chapel was opened in 1782 in Cherry Street, followed by others throughout the city. As the population of Birmingham grew, so too did the appeal of Non-conformism. Methodism soon outgrew its original town-centre chapel, and a new 1,100 seat hall was built just along the road from here near Old Square. Such was the strength of Methodism in Birmingham that this also rapidly became too small to accommodate the growing congregations, and this Central Hall was opened in 1903.

Soon cross over Newton Passage and continue along Corporation Street.

On the left are the Victoria Law Courts. Until 1884 all of Birmingham's major crimes were tried at Warwick, but in that year the city was granted the right to hold its own assizes. A law court was needed that would reflect the new-found grandeur of the city. It was initially planned that the Law Courts would be on the back of the Council House then being built in Victoria Square, but this plan was soon abandoned, the space being used for the Museum & Art Gallery (see Walk 10). Instead the Law Courts were built here. The courts were built between 1887–91, in the style of a French Renaissance chateau, using the red terracotta brick popular for many of Birmingham's civic buildings. The building was designed by Sir Aston Webb and Ingress Bell, with an imposing arched gated entrance reflecting the Arts and Crafts movement, and flanked by two huge towers. Inside is a Great Hall, the stained glass windows of which depict scenes from Birmingham's history. Look for the statue of Queen Victoria, by Walter Crane, over the entrance.

Opposite the Law Courts was the Salvation Army Citadel, built in 1891–92. The building, with its domed turrets, is still standing but is today used as offices. The Salvation Army was created in 1878 by William Booth, a former Methodist minister from Nottingham. Booth had begun working in the slums of London's East End in 1865, preaching to the very poor whom other religious orders ignored. It soon became apparent to him that prayer was not enough and that practical help was needed as well. He began a two-pronged attack, both upon the lack of religious faith among the homeless and destitute, and also upon the wretched social conditions in which they lived. For this he created the Salvation Army, with its military ranks, uniform and discipline and its desire to help those neglected by society. Soon Booth's work spread from London to other big cities, working wherever the poor lived in 'grim and godless' conditions. The citadel built here was the Army's headquarters in Birmingham.

Methodist Central Hall.

Follow the road as it bends left back on itself.

This road is Steelhouse Lane, its name reflecting the heavy industry that originally occupied this area. On your right is the Children's Hospital. The building was originally designed as Birmingham's General Hospital, in the city's trademark red terracotta brick, and opened in 1897. Although much redesigned, the original magnificent building can still be made out. It became a Children's Hospital in 1947.

Keep ahead up Steelhouse Lane, the police station on your left. Pass the other end of Newton Passage and keep ahead to Colmore Circus.

It is believed that this is the site of the 13th-century Priory, the Hospital of St Thomas of Canterbury. Historic records are hazy, and although it is known that the land from here south to beyond Old Square was owned by the Priory, the location of the actual building is a matter of speculation.

Cross to the middle of the sunken pedestrian amphitheatre of Colmore Circus, where new office blocks now stand. Turn right, and go through the circus, at right angles to the direction you

St Chad's, Britain's first Catholic cathedral since the Reformation.

entered. At a pedestrian crossing, leave the circus, cross the busy road and keep ahead down St Chad's Queensway, soon to reach St Chad's Circus.

St Chad's Roman Catholic Cathedral was designed by the famous architect Augustus Pugin in 1839. Its plain red-brick walls, steeply pitched roof and tall arcades are all in the style seen in 13th-century German churches. Pugin's aim was to create a full-blown Catholic church, mediaeval in appearance but located in a modern industrial setting from which all traces of the past have been obliterated. This style became known as 'Gothic Revival', of which St Chad's is a prime example. Inside is a pulpit from the Abbey of St Gertrude in Louvain, and a 15th-century German statue of the Virgin, donated by Pugin himself.

St Chad's was the first Catholic cathedral to be built in Britain since the Reformation. The Roman Catholic faith had initially been outlawed and, although discrete private worship was eventually tolerated, Roman Catholic services were not legally permitted until 1778, and Catholics were barred from public office for some years more. The growth of Catholicism in Birmingham reflected the large number of Irish immigrants who arrived in the town from the late 17th century onwards. The first Catholic church, St Peter's, was opened in Broad Street in 1786 in the heart of the Irish quarter. A second church, St Chad's, was built here in 1808, tightly crammed in among the factories and warehouses of the Gun Quarter, where many Catholics were employed. In 1841 Birmingham became the first Catholic diocese in England (64 years before the city became the centre of an Anglican diocese) and St Chad's was reconstructed as its cathedral.

From the front doors of St Chad's, turn right and leave St Chad's Circus by the subway. On the far side of the subway, turn right and follow the pavement into Great Charles Street Queensway. Follow the pavement through the underpass and then turn left into Livery Street. Walk up Livery Street to Colmore Row.

In the mid-19th century there was no national railway network, but instead a number of competing companies racing to cover as much of the country as possible, building railways that ran on different gauge tracks. The Great Western Railway Company, with tracks 7ft wide, reached Birmingham from the north-west in 1852 and built Snow Hill Station as a terminus. The London & North Western Railway pushed through a line from London two years later, using the more standard gauge of 4ft 8½ inches, opening New Street Station as its terminus. Although rail gauges were eventually standardised at the smaller

The original entrance to Snow Hill Station.

gauge, Snow Hill continued as a busy main line terminal until 1967. In that year the original Victorian station, together with a Great Western Hotel built on to its front, was demolished, and all main line services routed into New Street. Snow Hill subsequently reopened, and some inter-city services now run from it again.

All that remains of the original station is an arched doorway, halfway up Livery Street. Plans to redevelop the station include moving the entrance from its current position facing Colmore Row and reincorporating the Livery Street entrance into the design.

Cross Colmore Row at traffic lights and keep ahead into the Great Western Arcade.

The Great Western Arcade, first opened in 1874, is the best surviving example of the many shopping arcades built in late 19th-century Birmingham. It was originally two storeys high, with a balcony at the first floor and shops on both levels (the first floor was lost during the Blitz in World War Two). The construction of the arcade is a beautiful example of lateral thinking. A cutting had been dug to connect Snow Hill and New Street stations. In order to cut steam and noise pollution in the fashionable heart of the city, the cutting was roofed over, leaving an unsightly corridor of girdering and masonry at ground level. The solution – build a shopping arcade on top.

At the far end of the arcade cross Temple Row and continue ahead down North Western Arcade. At the far end turn right along Corporation Street.

In 1875, as part of the grandiose redevelopment of Birmingham's city centre planned by Joseph Chamberlain, areas of sub-standard housing were demolished in the city centre. A 'great street' was pushed through between 1879 and 1882, connecting New Street to the Priory Estate. This new road was modelled on a Parisian boulevard, 66ft wide and flanked with fine buildings in a mixture of styles deliberately chosen to challenge the classical tradition then prevalent in the city centre. It was estimated that to build the new road, which the City Corporation named 'Corporation Street' after themselves, would cost £1.5 million of ratepayers money, although it was planned that £1 million could be recouped by selling leases to retailers on what was to be Birmingham's premier shopping street. The remaining £½ million was termed 'a price well worth paying' for the creation of such a magnificent heart to the city.

Corporation Street remained the fashionable retail heart of Birmingham for the best part of a century. Although challenged by new retail developments in the High Street–Bull Ring area, especially the modern shopping arcades, it is still an important retail centre and preserves a certain elegance. Most of the original façades have gone at street level, replaced by the fascias of modern retailers, but look up to first-floor level as you walk along this street and the beautifully eclectic architecture of Chamberlain's great boulevard can still be seen.

Follow Corporation Street to a road junction with New Street.

New Street was first mentioned in 1397, as a well maintained (at least by mediaeval standards) road that led from the main Halesowen–Dudley road (to the west where Victoria Square now stands) to the top of the town, above the market square. This, the junction of modern New Street and Corporation Street, was the limit of the town in the Middle Ages. It was lined with a scattering of cottages and barns, and also one of Birmingham's oldest religious institutions.

Apart from the Priory, mediaeval Birmingham had two other religious orders in the vicinity of the town: one was the Guild of St John the Baptist at Deritland (see Walk 1), the other was the Guild of the Holy Cross, whose guild house stood here. Membership of the guilds was confined to the town's wealthiest citizens, and provided not only religious but also secular support, forerunners of modern social security and welfare benefits. The guilds also often ran schools for the children of their members. Both Birmingham's guilds were closed down during the Reformation, but the guildhall of the Guild of the Holy Cross was immediately refounded as King Edwards Grammar School. The timber-framed schoolhouse on this spot survived until 1707.

Later a toll house was built here, to collect revenue from travellers entering the town.

Later still, as the town grew, New Street became the fashionable street for shops, until superceded by the newly built Corporation Street in the late 19th century.

The entrance to New Street Station and the Pallisades Shopping Centre is up the ramp in front of you. To finish the walk, however, turn left in front of HSBC and walk along New Street. Turn right in front of Waterstones to return to the start.

Industry and transport: a walk along Birmingham's canals

The drive and energy of mediaeval Birmingham had enabled it to overcome its geographic disadvantages. Despite not being on an obvious natural routeway, such as a river, and despite having no raw materials nearby, it had built its prosperity upon trade and manufacturing. But by the early 18th century the roads and tracks leading into the town were unable to cope with the amount of traffic required. Although the introduction of turnpike roads improved matters for travellers, they were unsuitable for the bulk transportation of heavy goods. But then there occurred a revolution in transport. In 1761 the Duke of Bridgewater employed James Brindley, a millwright with no formal education, to construct a canal connecting his coalmines in Worsley to nearby Manchester. The success of the canal as a means of moving heavy goods quickly and cheaply was immediately apparent, and the next 60 years saw canals opened the length and breadth of England.

Birmingham manufacturers were quick to realise that canals would solve their problems, and could bring raw materials into the town and carry finished goods away to market very cheaply. In 1767 James Brindley was employed to cut a canal connecting the Black Country coalfields to Birmingham. The first barges loaded with Black Country coal arrived at wharfs in Newhall in November 1769. Birmingham's future as a major centre of heavy industry had arrived.

In the next few years a number of other canals were cut into Birmingham: the Birmingham and Fazeley Canal in 1783, the Birmingham and Worcester in 1791, the Birmingham and Warwick in 1793. These canals also provided access to a network of other canals and navigable rivers being developed across the country, and through them to ports. The Fazeley Canal led eventually to Liverpool and Hull, while the Warwick Canal led to London. From being a town built on an isolated plateau with difficult communications, Birmingham was now truly at the heart of England.

Start
This walk starts from Chamberlain Square.

With your back to the Chamberlain Memorial, climb the steps, passing between the statues of Watt and Priestley, and go through into the glass-fronted covered arcade ahead.

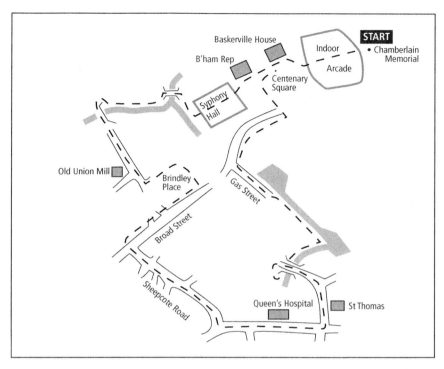

Two statues face down into Chamberlain Square, commemorating two engineers whose discoveries played an important part in the development of Birmingham industries. James Watt is shown with his hand resting upon a steam engine cylinder, in a statue made in 1868 by Alexander Munro. Opposite him is Francis Williamson's 1874 statue of Joseph Priestley (who discovered the properties of oxygen) shown concentrating on an experiment. Birmingham has always been proud of its engineering and manufacturing background, and has no problem using its civic art to commemorate men of science.

Go through the arcade to emerge on to Centenary Way. Follow the elevated walkway across the inner ring road to the Hall of Memory.

After World War One, a competition was held to design a suitable war memorial. In 1921 that competition was won by S.N. Cooke and W.N. Twist, who came up with the design for an octagonal, domed Hall of Memory. It is built out of Portland stone, a material not used in Birmingham until then, set upon a base of Cornish granite, to a design much cleaner and less cluttered than those employed in the Victorian era. Seated bronze figures on pedestals outside

Statue of Birmingham engineer James Watt.

The Hall of Memory, shrine to the dead of two world wars.

the building represent the armed services. The focus of the interior is a shrine, made of marble, on top of which is a bronze casket containing the roll of honour, wherein are listed the names of the Birmingham men who died in World War One.

Interior of the Hall of Memory.

The fourth design of Centenary Square, adopted in 1991.

Pass between the Hall of Memory on your left and Baskerville House on your right, then pause to look at Centenary Square.

The current Centenary Square is the last in a line of schemes for the area. As early as 1918 it was proposed that there would be a civic complex on this site, with exhibition halls, civic buildings and offices facing an open square. A plan of 1926 laid down the idea for a rectangular open area, aligned east–west along Broad Street, with buildings to three sides and open facing the road. This plan was abandoned as too expensive, although the orientation of the open square was retained. Further plans were adopted in 1944, these incorporating the newly built Baskerville House in the square's north-east corner, but these too were abandoned in 1948. A third, less formal layout was approved in 1958 but this too was never started. A fourth design was accepted in 1991, and this is the square we see today.

On your right is Baskerville House. The uncluttered lines of the Hall of Memory are picked up in its design, built between 1939–40 to a design by Cecil Howett. The building is somewhat classical in design, its monumental scale echoing the Town Hall but with far cleaner lines and made out of the same Portland stone and Cornish granite as the Hall of Memory. Baskerville House contained local council offices from 1940 until the end of the century. It is now being renovated as a hotel.

Baskerville House.

Further along on the right-hand side of the square is the Repertory Theatre, opened in 1990 and replacing the old theatre in Station Street (see Walk 8). It was highly controversial when it was built, very modern with a glass flattened curve façade and concrete fins projecting into the square. The magnificent main auditorium seats 1,200, and a smaller studio theatre seats a further 150, while bars and restaurants occupy the glass façade.

Facing you is the complex housing the Symphony Hall and International Conference Centre, opened in 1991. The purpose-built Symphony Hall, with seating capacity for 2,200, is now home to the Birmingham Symphony Orchestra, who moved here from the Town Hall, as well as providing a venue for a host of visiting artists, national and international. The ICC was a deliberate attempt to make Birmingham into an international business city. It consists of 12 halls arranged around a central mall, offering a range of first-rate conference facilities. Adjoining the ICC is the Hyatt Regency Hotel, with accommodation for 300 guests.

The square itself is grassed, with a prominent central water feature, a bronze and wire fountain. There was also, until 2005, a statue called the *Spirit of Enterprise*, a plaster and fibreglass representation of muscular workers from various of the city's industries, which proved very controversial due to its Stalinist style of sculpture. The statue was utterly destroyed by fire, not caused by a disgruntled art lover but by a teenage vandal.

The Symphony Hall and the Repertory Theatre.

Continue ahead along Centenary Square. Pass the Repertory Theatre on your right and keep ahead through the glass doors leading into the foyer of the Symphony Hall/ICC complex. Keep ahead along the broad walkway through the complex, a public right of way, descending steps to pass through a door on to the canal side, beside a statue.

The canal frontage here is a vivid illustration of Birmingham's regeneration. Until 25 years ago this area was a scene of industrial dereliction, a largely disused canal fronted by crumbling warehouses and abandoned industrial units. Today it is a vibrant area of cafés, restaurants and smart shops, with a complex of luxury apartments surrounding it, and with the canal towpath transformed into a pleasant promenade. The statue, *The Battle of the Gods and Giants*, by Roderick Tye, is intended to symbolise Birmingham's struggle to rebuild its centre.

The revitalised canal front in central Birmingham.

Brewmaster's House.

Turn right along the canal side, but first detour up the steps on your right to see the Brewmaster's House.

In its heyday in the 1790s 100 barges a day passed through the centre of Birmingham, bringing raw materials to its factories and taking finished goods to market. Each barge had a crew of up to six people, often members of the same family, engaged in the backbreaking work of moving the heavy canal boats, often as far as 30 miles a day. Naturally this was thirsty work, and a service industry grew up along the canalside to cater for the bargees' needs. A small brewery stood on this site, with the owner, who was also the master brewer, living here. This house, built around 1816, served both as the brewmasters home and as his office and retail outlet. Hops were delivered by canal barge to the brewery, and some of the beer produced was sold back to the bargees. To the rear is a beautifully restored cart shed, where the huge wagons or drays, used to transport casks of beer across the city, were stored.

Return to the canal and walk along the canal side walk, water on your left, soon passing the Malthouse Public House.

The Malthouse is a new pub, but its name reflects the fact that a brewery stood near this spot. The pub itself is built into the shell of the Kingston Building, built in 1803 as a nail warehouse. If you look back as you cross the small footbridge you can see the old warehouse frontage, with its high sashed windows. The remains of loading bays can also be seen: many warehouses were built facing directly on to the canals, with loading bays giving direct access to the barges.

Cross a footbridge in front of the NIA (National Indoor Arena) and turn left.

This is the junction of two canals, and the wide circle was not only to make it easy for barges to turn from one canal to the other, but also to provide a convenient turning spot, allowing barges to make the return trip. Going back the way you have just walked is the Worcester Canal, running for 30 miles to Worcester. It was opened in 1791 to connect Birmingham with the pottery towns of the West Midlands and from there to the Severn, with ultimate access to the Bristol Channel. There are 58 locks in the course of its 30 miles, allowing the canal to make the steep descent from the Birmingham plateau to the Severn basin. In one five-mile stretch there are 42 locks, lifting barges 300ft.

To your left and right is the Grand Union Canal. This canal was the brainchild of James Brindley, Britain's first canal builder, who conceived the idea of a 'grand

Junction of Worcester, Wolverhampton and Fazeley canals.

trunk' canal that would cross the whole of lowland England and link London, Bristol, Hull and Liverpool. A number of existing canals were to be linked to form one huge canal network. Although Brindley's grand concept was not fully realised, the main artery, linking London to Liverpool, was built and is known today as the 'Grand Union'. To your right the canal was originally the Fazeley Canal, opened in 1783, which in turn was connected to the Warwick Canal. Both were eventually incorporated into the Grand Union, which now runs for 124 miles to London, with two huge flights of locks, at Knole and at Hatton, to get barges off the canal, with further locks along its route.

To your left the canal, now also part of the Grand Union, runs 13 miles to Wolverhampton. The route is relatively flat, requiring only three locks in total. When it was cut, this was Birmingham's first canal, opened in 1772 to connect Birmingham with Wolverhampton and the Black Country, with its abundant raw materials. This canal played a vital part in the explosion of Birmingham's manufacturing industries in the latter part of the 18th century.

Follow the canal, the Sea Life Centre on the opposite side, soon passing under a footbridge.

This rather splendid wrought-iron footbridge was made in 1827 at the Horseley Iron Works in Stafford. The canal system linked the pottery towns with Wolverhampton and hence with Birmingham, and although no records exist it is likely that this bridge was transported down the canal from its Stafford foundry.

100 yards past the footbridge, turn right through a gate beside a plaque saying 'Canalside Walk, Sheepcote Street'. Immediately turn left and follow the pavement up to the road. Turn left over Sheepcote Street Bridge.

The name of this road gives echoes of a pre-industrial era. 'Sheepcote' is Anglo-Saxon meaning 'sheep cottages', and was the former home of shepherds who grazed their flocks here in the Middle Ages, in open pastures on top of the plateau, while Birmingham was still a small town huddled below the slopes a mile or so to the south.

Walk along Sheepcote Street where you will see new flats on both sides of you.

After the shepherds and their flocks were long gone, this area along Sheepcote Street, backing on to the main canal with its numerous spurs, was lined with

Brindley Place, symbol of Birmingham's urban regeneration.

warehouses and factories, teeming with life and industry in the 19th century. By the 1930s the area was in decline, with the canal no longer a convenient means of moving goods and materials and industry moving to better located sites further from the city centre. By the 1950s the area was in a seemingly terminal decline. However, the gentrification of the city centre in the 1990s gave the area a new lease of life. Today many of the old warehouses are luxury apartments, and the canals and docks provide walkways and promenades.

Cross the canal and in front of the Crescent Theatre cross the road at traffic lights. Turn right along Grosvenor Street West for 50 yards to see the Old Union Mill.

Although Birmingham is synonymous with manufacturing, there were many industrial units devoted to more domestic activities. Union Mill was built in 1813 and was the largest flour mill in the city. Its proximity to the canal network facilitated the bulk import of grain and the export of finished flour.

Return to Sheepcote Street, cross the road to the front of the Crescent Theatre again and turn right, passing along the front of the City Café. Turn left immediately past the café into Brunswick Square. Keep ahead, passing along a red-brick loggia, to enter Brindley Place.

Brindley Place, named after the father of canals James Brindley, lies at the heart of the redevelopment of Birmingham's dockland in the 1990s. It was laid out in 1995 to a design by Townsend Landscape Architects, combining walkways, sculptures and tree-surrounded pools in the midst of a complex of modern offices, shops, cafés and apartments. The buildings themselves, built mostly between 1996 and 1999, are all made from faced red brick and share a common size and design.

At the end of the red-brick loggia, with the green square on your left and fountains in front, turn right. Walk past the Ikon Gallery and follow the road out to Broad Street.

The Ikon Gallery occupies a building originally raised in 1877 as the Oozells Street School. Oozells Street, and the narrow side roads and alleys that ran off it, was home to a teeming population of recently settled migrant workers, attracted into the city by the prospect of work. The school was built for the children of the area, part of the enlightened policy of the City Fathers to provide educational opportunities for all. Although located in a poor working-class

The Ikon Gallery, built into a Victorian school.

district, the school was a splendid three-storey building in the Victorian Gothic style, designed by architects Martin & Chamberlain, who had been responsible for several of the important civic buildings in the city centre. As the area fell into disuse after World War Two and the original working-class population moved out, the school was closed. The building was renovated in 1997, with additional floors being put in, new wings added and the original tower (which had been removed in the 1960s) replaced. The exterior of the building, however, still retains much of its Victorian splendour.

Turn right along Broad Street. Pass the Novotel hotel, cross a side road at traffic lights and continue along Broad Street. Cross Sheepcote Street and pass in front of the Old Orleans bar.

The Old Orleans bar occupies a building originally built in 1815 as the Islington Glassworks. The canal is just behind it, providing easy transportation. In the very centre of the building, the three-storey, bay-windowed centrepiece was the owner's house. It was not unusual for factory owners in the early 19th century to have their houses built beside their factories, or even incorporated into the building itself. This enabled them to keep a close eye on their workforce and to pursue a very 'hands-on' style of management. It was not until well into the latter half of the century that factory owners felt the need to have a prestigious home some distance from the factory that provided them with their wealth.

Just past the Old Orleans bar cross Broad Street at pedestrian lights and then continue in the same direction along Broad Street, now on the opposite pavement. Just before the Cineworld Cinema, turn left into Bishopgate Street. Go along Bishopgate Street, soon crossing Tennant Street.

Unlike the Old Orleans, the City Tavern, on the corner of Tennant Street, was purpose built in 1901, in the red terracotta so symbolic of the civic buildings in Birmingham.

Continue along Bishopgate Street to its end, and there turn left into Bath Row. Follow Bath Row past the former Queen's Hospital.

Queen's Hospital was built in 1871–73, designed by Birmingham's great civic architects Martin & Chamberlain. It was a beautiful building with a romanesque façade, very Italian in appearance, and a high, arched, main

Ruins of St Thomas's Church, now a peace garden.

entrance. Now the hospital has largely been replaced by the complex of buildings called Queen's Hospital Close, and is part of the University of Birmingham.

In front of the former St Thomas's Church, now a peace garden, turn left into Granville Street.

St Thomas's was built in 1826–29, in a style known as Greek Revival. It had a tower, open to the nave on three sides, originally topped by a ball and cross, and a nave lined with Ionic columns. The church was largely destroyed in a bombing raid in 1941 and only the western end survived. The building was left as a ruin for several decades, until in 1992 it was decided to redesign the churchyard as a Peace Garden. The ruins of the church were incorporated into the layout, and serve as a poignant backdrop to the setting.

Follow Granville Street to a mini roundabout, and bear left with the road for 100 yards to reach a canal bridge. Cross the bridge and immediately turn left down steps on to the towpath. Turn left under the bridge and follow the towpath to reach a canal basin, with the Mailbox across the water on the right.

The Gas Street Basin.

The Mailbox was originally a postal sorting office, the largest in England, built in 1970. The building was left empty after the Post Office moved to new premises in the 1990s, and in 1999–2001 the building was converted into a complex of elegant shops, flats and hotels, lining a cavernous glass and concrete two-floor arcade that stretches back from the canal to Suffolk Street Queensway.

Turn left with the canal, soon reaching the Gas Street Basin.

The Gas Street Basin was at the centre of the network of interlocking canals that had been established, each by different companies, during the last quarter of the 18th century. Here there was a small basin on the Birmingham Canal (which was an extension of the original Birmingham to Wolverhampton Canal). In 1795 the Birmingham & Worcester Canal was dug through from the south to reach this basin, but so bitter was the rivalry between the two companies that a 7ft bar, still visible today, was left to separate the two canals. It was not until 1815 that a lock was cut, finally enabling north-south canal traffic to flow freely.

As soon as you reach the basin, turn left through an arch into Gas Street.

Facing you across Gas Street is Retort House, built in 1822 as the headquarters of the Birmingham Gas Light & Coke Company. The use of gas for lighting had been pioneered by Birmingham engineer William Murdock in 1795, when he was working as a mining engineer in Cornwall. Upon his return to Birmingham he continued his experiments with gas lighting and in 1802 publicly demonstrated his invention by illuminating his factory. The idea of street lighting, powered by gas, was soon accepted by the Street Commissioners, a body of 50 leading citizens who ran the town of Birmingham until the Corporation was set up in 1851.

The Birmingham Gas Light & Coke Co. was formed with the purpose of supplying the city with gas, importing coal by canal to the Gas Basin, where it was converted in nearby huge retorts into coke and gas. The retorts stood behind the headquarters building, lining the road still named Gas Street, and have long since disappeared, although a coal store can still be seen adjoining the building. Given the volatile nature of gas production, there was obviously a major risk of fire. To make the headquarters as fireproof as possible, the building was constructed with cast-iron columns and wrought-iron tie rods to support the brick walls, topped with a roof constructed from iron girders upon which slates were laid.

For the first few years, the Birmingham Gas Light & Coke Co. was immensely profitable, the sole supplier of gas for lights which were soon to be seen in nearly every street in the town. But in 1825 the Staffordshire Gas Light Co. was formed, to supply gas to much of the Black Country and to light the roads leading into Birmingham. Strong rivalry developed between the two companies, with intense political lobbying of the Street Commissioners and other leading citizens, the result of which was that in 1845 the Staffordshire Gas Light Co. was awarded the contract to supply gas to almost the whole of Birmingham. The Birmingham Gas Light & Coke Co. went into rapid decline, and was eventually bought out by its rival.

The Staffordshire Gas Light Co. held on to its lucrative monopoly for another 30 years, before it was taken over by Birmingham Corporation in 1875, part of Joseph Chamberlain's drive to bring all the city's public services under municipal control (see Walk 10).

Turn right along Gas Street.

Most of the buildings that line Gas Street date from the 19th century. Almost immediately you pass No. 46 Gas Street, on your right. This was the office of the Worcester & Birmingham Canal Company. Just beyond this, on the left, is the white-plastered building that today houses the headquarters of Carlton TV. The building itself was originally a factory, with incorporated factory owner's house, dating from 1821.

Follow Gas Street to junction with Broad Street.

Opposite you is the Brasshouse, today a pub/restaurant, but housed in a building from 1781 which, as the name suggests, was once a brassworks. Although Birmingham was already manufacturing brassware by the early 18th century, it was the arrival of the canal that really allowed the brass industry to take off. Heavy raw materials could now be imported cheaply, while much larger brass goods, including cannon, could be manufactured and then sent cheaply to market.

Turn right along Broad Street, soon reaching the garish golden statue to Boulton, Watt and Murdock.

The bronze statue, a 1956 work by William Bloye, commemorates three of Birmingham's greatest industrialists.

Matthew Boulton was born in Birmingham and was the son of a toy manufacturer (in the 18th century 'toys' were not simply or even mainly children's

Statue to Boulton, Watt and Murdock, fathers of Birmingham's industry.

toys, but any small ornamental objects. Buckles and buttons were among the main 'toys' produced in Birmingham at that time). After his father's death in 1759, Matthew took over the family business in the vicinity of Snow Hill. Boulton was a shrewd entrepreneur, who set about expanding his business. He entered into partnership with John Fothergill and, while John travelled Europe bringing in new customers, Matthew set about building useful contacts among the nobility of Europe. An inlaid sword was presented to the future George III and Count Orloff (the favourite of Catherine the Great of Russia) was conducted around the Snow Hill factory, as was the nephew of the King of Poland.

In 1761 Boulton relocated his business to larger premises at Handsworth, a combined factory and showroom, with accommodation for the workforce on the top floor. Boulton was an enlightened employer, providing clean and hygienic working conditions and a subsidised insurance scheme for his workers. In this factory, named the Soho Works, were produced luxury items such as gilded brass ornaments and silver plated tableware. By 1775 Boulton was Birmingham's major manufacturer, but in that year his business took another major leap forward when he entered into partnership with a Scottish engineer eight years his junior, James Watt.

James Watt had been born in Glasgow in 1736, an engineer by trade, who had in 1769 patented a much improved design of steam engine for use in the mining industry, where there was the constant need to pump water out of deep mines.

Yet by 1773 Watt was in financial difficulties, and he left his native Glasgow to chance his fortune in Birmingham. Matthew Boulton had already expressed interest in Watt's invention, and in 1775 the two men entered a partnership, not only to manufacture steam engines, but also to develop them so that they could be used in factory manufacturing processes. Boulton now built another factory, the Soho Foundry, to build steam engines, and by 1800 Boulton and Watt had installed some 450 steam engines nationwide.

William Murdock, another Scot, had moved to Birmingham in 1777 when he was only 23. He soon found work with Boulton and Watt, supervising the installation and running of steam engines in the tin and copper mines of Cornwall. Murdock soon saw the potential of steam engines, not merely to drive pumps and machines, but also as a form of transport. Sometime in the early 1780s Murdock built a tiny model of a locomotive but neither Watt (who seemed to feel threatened by his employee) nor Boulton encouraged its development, and steam locomotion had to wait 30 years for George Stevenson. Instead Murdock, still based in Cornwall, turned his attention to the potential use of coal gas for lighting. When he returned to Birmingham in 1798 he continued his experiments in Boulton's Soho Works. By 1802 he was in a position to demonstrate the potential of gas lighting which, as we have seen, was soon adopted by the Street Commissioners to light Birmingham. Murdock later went on to pioneer a form of gas-fired central heating.

Boulton and Watt, who had already ignored Murdock's ideas for steam locomotives, also failed to develop his ideas for street lighting, which were left to other companies. Instead they continued to build engines, mainly for steam boats. Matthew Boulton died in 1809 and James Watt followed him in 1819. Both were buried in Handsworth Church. The companies they had founded went into decline and closed in 1848. Murdock died in 1839 and was buried in Handsworth Church, next to his employers.

In front of the statue, cross Broad Street at traffic lights to get back into Centenary Square. Turn right back to the start.

Walk 7

The Newhall Estate and the growth of the Jewellery Quarter

In the Middle Ages the land to the north of present day Colmore Row was owned by St Thomas's Priory. With the Dissolution of the Monasteries the land was acquired by the Colmore family. They built a fine house, New Hall, in the centre of the estate, which for the next 200 years remained a mixture of farming and parkland, well to the north of the town of Birmingham. By the early 18th century the expansion of the town had reached the edge of the estate, and in 1746 Anne Colmore started to parcel her lands out for development. Each plot was sold on a 120-year lease, and Anne obtained an Act of Parliament, making these leases binding upon her successors. The plots were laid out around a grid pattern of streets, and by the 1750s building work was well under way to create an estate of fine town houses. In 1777 Charles Colmore donated further land in the north-west corner of the estate, where St Paul's Church now stands, to encourage further development in that direction. By 1810 almost the whole area of the Newhall estate was covered with substantial town houses with private gardens.

Industry was soon to arrive in the Newhall Estate. The digging of branches of the Birmingham canal through the estate made the carriage of raw materials

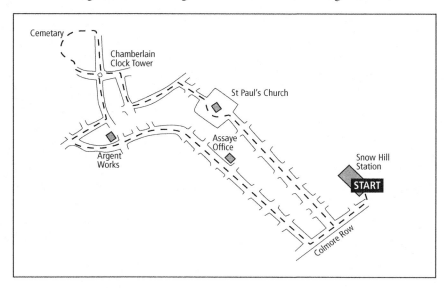

and finished goods easier. Isolated factories grew up, where the metal trinkets and boxes for which Birmingham was becoming famous were manufactured. By the middle of the 19th century precious metal trades were migrating from the rest of Birmingham and concentrating in this area. The Jewellery Quarter had been born.

Start

This walk starts at the main entrance to Snow Hill Station, on to Colmore Row.

With your back to Snow Hill Station, turn right along Colmore Row. Cross over Livery Street and continue along Colmore Row, soon passing St Phillip's Cathedral on your left.

You are walking along what, in 1746, was the boundary of the New Hall estate. To your right was the high wall surrounding the parkland, orchards and fields of the estate. To your left stood the new church of St Phillip's, consecrated in 1715. To the left of the church, behind the present-day North Western Arcade, was the gentrified area of the Priory Estate (see Walk 5), completed around 1700. Beyond St Phillip's and facing the church, fine new houses were being built on the top of the slope (see Walk 10). The original town of Birmingham, crowded, noisy and dirty, was down the slope beyond, towards St Martin's Church. What is now Colmore Row was in 1746 a muddy country lane, called New Hall Lane, running through fields and open pasture and linking the Lichfield and Dudley roads out of the city. The lane was renamed Colmore Row, after the Colmore family gave the New Hall estate over to development in 1746, and buildings started to go up on the northern side of the road (your right as you are walking) almost immediately. However, there was no building along the southern (left as you are walking) side of Colmore Row beyond St Phillip's until 1823.

Cross over Church Street on your right. At traffic lights turn right into Newhall Street.

The original buildings on this side of Colmore Row, built in the 1750s, were redeveloped from 1869 onwards, with grander and more elaborate buildings replacing the smaller town houses of the Newhall estate development. On the street corner on the right was the Union Club (now Bamfords Trust House) with carved heads over the windows staring ferociously at passers-by. The Union Club in its present form is the work of Yeoville Thomason, designer of

Carved heads stare down from the former Union Club.

the Council House, built in 1869 and one of the first buildings in the redevelopment of Colmore Row.

The Union Club was a private club for members of the highly influential Birmingham Political Union (BPU). The BPU had been founded in 1830, to campaign for parliamentary reform. At that time the distribution of parliamentary seats was outdated and grossly unfair. Small villages with less than a dozen households could elect a member of Parliament, and in one notorious example a borough with no inhabitants at all could still return an MP, but Birmingham, with a population of 85,000, was unrepresented. A campaign to get an MP for Birmingham had started in 1817, led by Thomas Attwood, partner in one of the city's leading banks. Under Attwood's energetic guidance the campaign continued, gradually broadening its targets to include the wider issue of Parliamentary reform. The BPU was founded in 1830 with Attwood as its president. It claimed to be a 'general political union between the lower and the middle classes' and soon had over 9,000 members. Similar organisations were springing up across the country, organising petitions and mass rallies. The culmination of their efforts was to be the Reform Bill of 1832, which saw a limited redistribution of parliamentary seats, including two for Birmingham, but which was the first step along the road which was eventually to lead to universal suffrage.

Thomas Attwood, and the BPU's vice-president Joshua Scholefield, were elected as Birmingham's first two MPs in December 1832. Attwood held his seat

Newhall Street, now a busy road but once the formal drive leading to New Hall.

until 1839, when ill-health forced him to resign. The BPU continued to flourish throughout the 19th century, playing its part in campaigning for the second and third Reform Bills.

Go down Newhall Street.

This long straight road follows the course of the entrance drive to New Hall. In 1746 there were imposing gates at the entrance to the estate, where the Union Club now stands. The broad drive descended, arrow-straight, across the parkway towards New Hall itself, which stood behind where Baker & Finmore (the white building seen ahead where the road bends left) now stands. None of the roads and buildings we now see were here in 1746: instead, there was open grassy parkland, with orchards off to the right, and with New Hall dominating the vista. New Hall was a large, three-storey building, with a central pediment over an imposing doorway, flanked by two projecting wings. The hall was demolished in 1787.

Cross over Great Charles Street Queensway at traffic lights and continue down Newhall Street.

Even after the development of the Newhall Estate for houses after 1746 this area at the bottom of Newhall Hill remained open land, on which fairs were occasionally held. It was the ideal spot for public meetings, and mass meetings demanding parliamentary reform had been held here in 1817 and 1819. As the campaign for the Reform Bill got under way, organised by the Birmingham Political Union, Newhall Hill was again chosen for a political rally. On 3 October 1831 church bells rang out across the city, inviting people to the largest rally Birmingham had ever seen. Over 100,000 attended to demonstrate their support for the Reform Bill then passing through Parliament. But the Bill was defeated by the House of Lords, and in May 1832 a second rally was called as part of a nationwide demonstration of support for the Bill. This time nearly 200,000 demonstrators turned up at Newhall Hill, a scene repeated across the country. This time the Bill passed into law.

Cross over Lionel Street and continue along Newhall Street.

On the right-hand corner of Charlotte Street is the Assay Office. During the course of the 18th century the jewellery trade became established in Birmingham, whose craftsmen developed a worldwide reputation for working in precious metals. Central to that reputation was the quality control of the goods produced, which needed to be officially tested and hallmarked by government-licensed employees. Initially goods had to be sent elsewhere, often as far as London, for 'assaying' or testing, but Matthew Boulton, one of Birmingham's leading industrialists, campaigned for the city to have its own assaying facilities. The first Assay Office was opened in New Street in 1773 and operated for over a century. As the jewellery trade became concentrated in the Jewellery Quarter, there was an increasing demand for the Assay Office to be located within the quarter itself, and it finally moved here in 1877.

On your left is the former Science Museum. The bay-windowed building, built on the bank of the Digbeth branch canal, was originally the factory of G.R. Elkington, one of the many self-taught craftsmen of Birmingham, who pioneered the process of electro-plating. As his business expanded, Elkington moved into this factory in 1850 and continued to trade from here until his death in 1865. As well as being a leading industrialist, Elkington was an art collector and helped fund the building of Birmingham's Art Gallery and the purchase of the paintings displayed within it. Elkington also helped to put on the 'Exhibition of the Manufactures of Birmingham and the Midland Counties' in 1849. This combined the display of works of art with a major exhibition of the range and innovative design of goods made in the city and attracted visitors from across Britain and beyond, including Prince Albert. A showcase for design and industry, the Exhibition's themes were taken up in the Great Exhibition of 1851 in London's Crystal Palace. Although the Birmingham Exhibition was temporary, many of its exhibits and themes were retained as the basis of the Science Museum, which was fittingly housed in Elkington's old factory after his death.

The Museum of Science & Industry moved into new, purpose-built premises incorporated into the Millenium Point complex when it opened in 2001 (see Walk 1).

Cross over the crossroads with George Street and Brook Street, and keep ahead, bearing left with the road (now Graham Street) in front of Baker & Finnemore Ltd.

You are now standing roughly where New Hall was located. Pause for a moment and look back. In 1746 none of the roads and buildings you see would have existed. Instead parkland, with fields and orchards off to the left, would have risen gently to the skyline.

Continue up Graham Street, passing Sovereign Court on your right and a Sikh temple on your left.

The building that now houses the Ramgarhia Sikh Temple was built in 1844 as the Highbury Independent Chapel. With its classical frontage, round-headed windows and projecting centre, it is one of the finest examples of a 19th-century Non-conformist chapel left in the city. The majority of the craftsmen and artisans who moved into the Jewellery Quarter were not native brummies, and many of them were political or religious Non-conformists. They were enticed into the city not only by the freedom to work without restriction, but also by the more liberal atmosphere in Birmingham (see Walk 5). Non-conformist chapels were established wherever the new immigrants settled. As the original community moved on, and the popularity of their religion declined, the chapel became home to the religious beliefs of a later influx of immigrants.

Follow Graham Street to the crossroads with Frederick Street and Newhall Hill.

On the right-hand corner closest to you is the Victoria Works, while facing it across the side road is the Argent Centre. Small factories such as these, employing only a small workforce, were typical of the work units that grew up in the Jewellery Quarter in the 19th century, and reflect the diversity of manufacturing in the area.

The Victoria Works was built in 1839–40 for Joseph Gillott, whose business was the manufacture of pen-nibs. It was one of the first purpose-built factories in the Jewellery Quarter. The total process of manufacture took place in this one factory, from the arrival of the sheet metal to the output of nibs of many different shapes and sizes, the task being broken down into numerous small steps, each step undertaken by specialised groups of skilled workers. Boys would enter the factory, often as young as 14, and learn 'on the job' as apprentices to older workers, gradually acquiring skills that they would employ throughout their working lives. It was not infrequent for men to stay in the same factory from boy to retirement. Nibs from this factory, 100 million a year in 1853, were sold worldwide, servicing the seemingly inexhaustible demand created by ever growing literacy. Joseph Gillott was typical of many manufacturers in the Midlands, developing tremendous expertise in a very specialised niche market, a market of such size that he never needed to diversify into other products.

The Argent Centre was built in 1862–63 to house Wiley's pen works. While Gillott concentrated upon the manufacture of pen-nibs, Wiley manufactured the pens themselves, employing the same production methods and a similarly highly skilled and specialised workforce.

Both factories, but especially the Argent Centre, are not merely functional, but were also built to be architecturally impressive. In particular, look at the tall Italianate windows of the Argent Centre, with surrounding red, white and blue

Elaborate brickwork on the Argent Centre.

brick details. Hollow bricks with metal reinforcements were used to support additional storeys without adding too much unsightly bulk. Look also at the large curved pediment above the Victoria Works, decorated with a medallion of Queen Victoria. For Victorian manufacturers, their factories were not merely the places that created their wealth, but they were also a reflection of their pride in their achievement and a demonstration of the self-confidence of the age they lived in.

Keep ahead up Legge Lane, bearing right to pass Camden drive on the left and soon passing the dilapidated Wellington Works on your left.

Although the Wellington Works is now a ruin, echoes of its former glory can still be made out, especially in the red and blue brick surrounds to the windows. The works was opened in 1879, for the manufacture of pencils.

Bear right with Legge Lane, with the ornate Manton building, in front of you.

The Manton factory was opened in 1834 and specialised in the manufacture of silver and cut-glass products. While the factories we have passed so far mass-produced highly specialised but comparatively low unit priced goods, the Manton factory concentrated on a more limited output of highly priced ornaments. Mr Manton was one of the first craftsmen to open a factory in Birmingham to service the increasing demand for expensive ornaments among Britain's growing upper-middle classes.

On the right-hand side of the road is Alabaster & Wilson's jewellery factory, opened 60 years after the Manton's factory in 1892. By then the worldwide demand for Birmingham jewellery was such that small-scale domestic production by individual artisans could no longer keep up with that demand, and larger jewellery-producing units were being built. They still employed skilled craftsmen, requiring a lengthy apprenticeship, but the work was now done in a factory setting, with workers often now undertaking one part in the process rather than seeing an individual product through from beginning to end.

Today Legge Lane and the surrounding streets have a rather run-down air, but in the 19th century it was a vibrant bustling neighbourhood with small factories producing a diverse range of well-crafted products that were in demand across the world, while the surrounding streets housed the skilled workers employed in those factories. Frequently, several generations of the same family were employed in the same industry, often in the same factory, with specialised skills passing from father to son.

Factory houses along Albion Street.

Follow Legge Lane to a crossroads and turn right into Albion Street. Go along Albion Street, passing Tenby Street on the left.

Although during the 19th century some manufacturing was done in purpose-built factories, much was carried out by individual artisans working either out of their own homes or out of rooms hired in other peoples homes. There are a number of 'factory houses' along Albion Street, especially on the right-hand side. Look for Nos 58–61: these were two pairs of houses, entered from a central passageway via a side door, with two-storey workshops to the rear and living accommodation for the family at the front. They were built around 1839, and were occupied by a skilled craftsman and his family. The artisan would have hand-made jewellery, often aided in the less skilled work by other members of his family, and either sold the finished product to middle-men or directly to the public, for which purpose the front downstairs room was often set up as a shop front. The houses to both sides were also factory houses, Nos 54–57 dating from the same time, Nos 62–65 some 40 years later. A number of small independent businesses still trade from these houses, although few are actually lived in any longer.

At a T-junction turn left along Frederick Street.

Frederick Street, especially on the left-hand side, has many more examples of factory houses, some of which have been knocked through to create small factories.

Although today Albion Street and Frederick Street contain many of the best surviving factory houses, in the 19th-century heyday of the Jewellery Quarter many streets were lined with houses that each had their own workshop. Until the latter half of the century, the majority of skilled jewellery production was carried out by artisan families working for themselves out of workshops incorporated into the family home. Gradually, economies of scale led to an increasing proportion of manufacturing to be done in purpose-built factories, with independent artisans replaced by waged workers, but the tradition of the independent craftsman still survives in the quarter.

Follow Frederick Street to a busy crossroads, with the Chamberlain Clock Tower standing in the middle of the junction.

This crossroads is the very centre of the Jewellery Quarter, and the ornate clock tower standing in the middle of the road was erected in 1903 to commemorate the return of Joseph Chamberlain from South Africa. Chamberlain was Birmingham's first mayor from 1873 to 1876, during which time he laid the foundations for the city as we know it today (see Walk 10). He entered Parliament in 1876 as a liberal, joined the Conservatives in 1895 and served as Colonial Secretary from 1895 until 1902, when his handling of affairs in southern Africa was highly controversial. Chamberlain was a convinced imperialist and had no sympathy for demands from the Boers, settlers of Dutch origin, for

The Chamberlain Clock Tower, erected in honour of Joseph Chamberlain.

independence from Britain. Far from negotiating a peaceful solution to the problem, Chamberlain allowed a number of highly aggressive actions to be undertaken against the Boers. The most notable was the Jameson Raid of 1895, when an armed British force entered the Dutch colony of Transvaal in an attempt to overthrow the government. This raid soured relations between the British Government and the Boers, culminating in the outbreak of the Boer War in 1899. Although a Parliamentary Commission exonerated Chamberlain, it was widely believed that he had foreknowledge of the conspiracy to overthrow the Transvaal government.

When the war ended in 1902 with the secession of the Boer Republics of Transvaal and Orange Free State, Chamberlain personally visited the remaining British territory of South Africa, launching the policy of 'Imperial Preference', which gave preferential trade deals to Britain's colonies and was designed to strengthen the economic bonds of the Empire. The city of Birmingham, staunchly unionist in politics, celebrated the return of its favourite son from South Africa with this tower.

Turn left along Warstone Lane for 50 yards to reach the ornate gatehouse of a cemetery.

The ornate gatehouse to the Church of England cemetery was built in 1848 by architects Hamilton and Medland, who were strongly influenced by the work of

Ornate gatehouses leading into the Jewellery Quarter's graveyard.

Sunken graveyard, with entrances to tombs in the side walls.

Augustus Pugin, the leading architect of the day. It is in an elaborate Gothic style, built from blue Staffordshire stone, with an oriel window above the arch. By 1848 the existing graveyards in the centre of Birmingham were becoming badly overcrowded, causing a public health hazard as well as inconvenience. This cemetery was opened on empty land just beyond the encroaching sprawl of housing to provide much-needed burial space. When Christ Church in New Street was demolished in 1899 the 600 bodies in its graveyard were transferred here in long convoys of hearses travelling at night to avoid disturbing the living inhabitants of the city.

Enter the churchyard by a path to the left of the archway and follow a broad gravelled path through the graveyard.

On the left is a sunken amphitheatre, made inside an early 19th-century sandpit, which contains a second tier of the graveyard. A chapel, demolished in 1954, stood on the rim of the amphitheatre. There are catacombs dug into the hillside around the amphitheatre (the entrances can be seen in the retaining wall), to provide yet more burial space. Today the cemetery has a rather run-down air to it, but it is worth exploring for its fine examples of Victorian funereal architecture.

On reaching the road on the far side of the churchyard turn right for 50 yards to a T-junction.

To visit the Jewellery Quarter Museum, turn left for a quarter of a mile, passing the Metro Station. The museum is housed in an 1899 jewellery workshop and tells the story of jewellery manufacture in Birmingham.

The Museum is open 9.15am (10.15am at weekends) until 4pm, Tuesday to Sunday. Admission is free.

To continue the walk, turn right back to the clock tower. At the clock tower turn left for 50 yards, then turn right into Vittoria Street. Walk along Vittoria Street.

On the right-hand side of the road is the School of Jewellery & Silversmithing. This was founded in 1888 and moved into the present building in 1890. By the 1880s the Jewellery Quarter had established a worldwide reputation for the excellence of its design and manufacture, but skills were still learnt on the job, either through formal apprenticeships in the factories or passed down from father to son in the workshops. Under Chamberlain and his successors, schooling was a matter of civic pride and formal education for the workers of Birmingham was a priority. The establishment of a school to formally teach the skills necessary for working in jewellery manufacture was part of this drive, and the School of Jewellery & Silversmithing has flourished to this day. Today the school is part of the University of Central England.

At a displaced crossroads, with the Regent works on the corner to your right, turn left along Regent Place.

There are many fine examples of small factories and factory houses along Regent Street. No. 16 Regent Street, a typical factory house, has been put under the control of English Heritage, and there are plans to restore it to its 19th-century condition and open it to the public as a living museum.

At the next crossroads turn right along Caroline Street to reach St Paul's Square.

The church of St Paul's was designed by architect Roger Eykyns and built in 1777–79. Elkins's design was inspired by St Martin's in the Fields in London. The building has a rectangular nave, with the altar in a rectangular apse. Inside

St Paul's Church.

the nave are five bays, with pillars supporting a gallery, from which in turn imposing Ionic pillars sweep up to a barrel ceiling. The 18th-century box pews still survive. At the eastern end is a fine stained-glass window designed in 1785 by Francis Eginton, which was inspired by Benjamin West's painting *The conversion of St Paul*. The tower was added in 1823 to the west end of the church, with two flanking vestries being built at the same time.

The site for St Paul's Square was donated by Charles Colmore. The square was developed at the same time as the church, with fine town houses facing into the green central square and the church. It is the only truly Georgian square in the city.

Go through the square, passing St Paul's on your left, and keep ahead along Ludgate Hill opposite. Follow Ludgate Hill to cross the busy Great Charles Street Queensway by a footbridge, and then continue up Church Street. At the top of Church Street turn left along Colmore Row to return to the start of the walk.

Walk 8

Migrants and Music Halls: a walk around the Holloway

This is very much a walk of two halves, the first part being through the heart of Birmingham's theatre land, and then going through the streets that surround Holloway Circus, home to waves of Birmingham's immigrants over the centuries.

During the early years of the 19th century, industry expanded dramatically in Birmingham. A long tradition of manufacturing and skilled craftsmanship was combined with the innovations of the Industrial Revolution to make Birmingham into the foremost manufacturing town in Victorian England. Factories arose on every side, creating a seemingly inexhaustible demand for labour. At the same time, modernisation of long-established agricultural methods led to huge numbers of rural labourers becoming redundant, and many of these flocked to nearby cities such as Birmingham in search of work. In the decade 1841–51 the population of Birmingham went up by 22 per cent,

as migrants from the countryside were swelled by immigrants from abroad, initially Irish fleeing poverty and famine at home. Other nationalities moved into the city as the decades progressed, from the Indian sub-continent, from China and elsewhere. The streets around Holloway Circus became home to successive nationalities, and their traces are still in evidence.

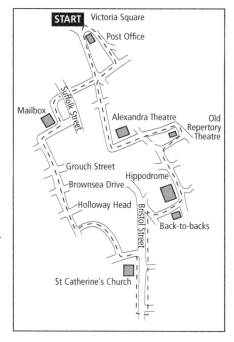

As the population and the prosperity of Birmingham expanded, so did the demand for entertainment. Music hall was a highly popular form of entertainment in the first half of the 19th century, and although many were converted to cinemas in the early 20th century, several of the variety theatres that grew out of the

Anthony Gormley's statue The Iron Man, symbolising Birmingham's industry.

music hall tradition still flourish and are to be found in the part of the city designated in 1905 as Birmingham's Theatreland.

Start

This walk starts from the Central Post Office, on the southern side of Victoria Square.

Face the Post Office, with your back to Victoria Square, beside an imposing piece of modern sculpture.

The 12ft high sculpture is *The Iron Man*, created by Anthony Gormley in 1992. A human torso, enclosed in iron beams, it symbolises the industrial tradition of Birmingham.

Walk down Pinfold Street, keeping the Post Office on your right hand. At the bottom of Pinfold Street, opposite the entrance to New Street Station, turn right into Navigation Street. Keep ahead for 50 yards to reach traffic lights. Cross the road at the lights, cross again over Hill Street, and then turn left along the pedestrianised John Bright Street, the Gala Casino on your left-hand side. Follow John Bright Street, passing the closed-down Futurist cinema.

The Futurist cinema was opened in 1920, a very imposing building that reflects the importance of cinema at that time. Until the end of the 19th century live theatre, and especially the music hall, were the main source of entertainment in Birmingham, but as the new century dawned so did the popularity of a new form of entertainment, the 'moving picture'. The first cinemas were made from converted music halls, but in 1910 the first purpose-built cinemas opened in the city. The growth in popularity of this new form of entertainment was rapid – in 1911 there were seven cinemas in

Birmingham, by 1914 that number had grown to 53, and by 1939 there were nearly 100. The Futurist was built with the red and cream terracotta brick so typical of Birmingham, but has more classical lines than most of the city's civic architecture and, with its columned arcade above the entrance, the building was seen as an important piece of architecture as well as a place of entertainment.

Continue along John Bright Street, soon to reach the Alexandra Theatre on your left.

The Alexandra was opened in 1901, originally as the Lyceum but soon renamed in honour of Edward VII's queen. From the outset it saw its role as the presentation of plays of popular appeal, in contrast to the more 'highbrow' productions in the nearby Repertory Theatre. Musicals, light operetta and variety shows were its forte, and since the Theatre Royal closed in 1956 it has been the city's principal venue for pantomime.

Today it often hosts large-scale touring productions.

Turn left with the road, the NCP in front of you, passing the Victoria public house on the corner.

Despite the strong influence of Methodism upon the working classes of Birmingham, public houses have always flourished in the city. The Victoria, opened in 1883 and named in honour of Queen Alexandra's predecessor, is a fine example of the grand inner-city pubs that were built during the later half of the 19th century.

Follow the road out to a crossroads. Keep ahead along the continuation of Station Street, passing the Crown Inn on the corner and soon passing the Old Repertory Theatre on your right.

Today Station Street is run down, but in its hey-day it was rather splendid, central to the city and lined with fine buildings, whose main function was to provide entertainment for the citizens of Birmingham. The Repertory Theatre (now prefixed by 'Old' to distinguish it from its modern successor on Chamberlain Square) was the finest building on the street. Its Classical pilasters, Greek-style friezes, large ornate windows and end towers make it a serious and imposing building, and reflect its role as the purveyor of serious and imposing theatre, not the more frivolous music hall that previously dominated the live entertainment scene in Birmingham.

The Old Repertory Theatre, Station Street.

By 1907 Birmingham had an established repertory company, the Pilgrim Players, who had no theatre of their own but instead performed at venues across the city. In 1912 theatrical entrepreneur Sir Barry Jackson, who was committed to producing high drama not light entertainment, conceived the idea of a permanent home for the company in a purpose-built theatre dedicated to serious drama. The Repertory Theatre opened the following year with a production of Shakespeare's *Twelfth Night*. For 20 years Sir Barry managed the Repertory Theatre, ensuring it stayed true to its original concept with ambitious programmes of plays by leading playwrights, even if this meant running at a financial loss at times, a loss Sir Barry covered from his own pocket. Even after the Repertory Theatre became a Trust in 1934 and Sir Barry gave up his control, he still played a major role in the running and programming of the Rep, right up to his death in 1961. The theatre was highly influential in both the work it produced and the calibre of actors who trained there, including Laurence Olivier, Noel Coward and Peggy Ashcroft.

The Birmingham Repertory Company eventually transferred to the new purpose-built theatre in Chamberlain Square, opened in 1991 (see Walk 6). It was by then the longest-surviving repertory company in England. The 'Old Rep', as it is known, continues to function as a theatre.

Turn right with the road and then turn right again along Hinckley Street. At the end of the road, opposite the Albany Banqueting Suite, turn left down to traffic lights. Cross over the dual carriageway and keep ahead. Where the road bends left, cross at pedestrian lights and keep ahead along a short stretch of pedestrianised road, passing the Hippodrome on your right.

The building today occupied by the Birmingham Hippodrome was built in 1895 as an Assembly Rooms, a suite of meeting rooms that could be let out to local groups and clubs. Four years later a 'Tower of Varieties' was added to the back of the building, a large hall containing a combination of stage and circus ring. A miniature version of Blackpool Tower was built on to the roof to advertise the new theatre. It was envisaged that elaborate variety shows could be performed at the new Tower of Varieties and travelling circuses would perform there, but the venture was not a success and folded within 12 months. In 1900 the building was taken over and reopened as the Trivoli Theatre, still sporting its distinctive tower. The theatre was renamed the Hippodrome in 1903.

In its early years the Hippodrome hosted variety shows and travelling musical events, but it gradually become one of the city's cultural centres. In a bold move, designed to bring 'high culture' to the provinces, the Sadler's Wells

Ballet Company moved from London in the early 1980s, renamed themselves the Birmingham Royal Ballet and made the Hippodrome their home. The Welsh National Opera followed suit, making the Hippodrome their second home.

The theatre was reconstructed several times and the tower was eventually taken down in 1963. The auditorium was rebuilt in 1925, there was extensive rebuilding of the stage, dressing rooms and backstage areas when Sadler's Wells moved up in 1980 and the Assembly Rooms were finally replaced with a new frontage, foyer and studios in 2001. The original 1899 side wall can still be seen around the corner in Inge Street.

Turn right along Inge Street, passing the Back-to-Back Museum on your left.

The upsurge in industry in Birmingham in the early 18th century led to a rapid rise in population as migrants swarmed into the city, attracted by the prospects of comparatively well-paid employment. This led to massive pressure on housing. An ingenious answer to the housing shortage was back-to-backs. Terraces of two or usually three-storey buildings went up, with usually only two rooms per floor, built in square city blocks. A further terrace was built on to the

back of the street-facing terrace, sharing a common back wall. These interior terraces faced on to a courtyard in the centre of the block, in the centre of which was an open courtyard. The courtyard contained a water pump, toilets and a communal wash house, and it served all the families who lived in the block, both those facing the street and those facing the courtyard. As this was often as many as 40 families, the minimal facilities were stretched to capacity. Inhabitants drew up strict rotas for the use of the wash-house, and there was considerable peer pressure to keep the toilets and

Entrance to a courtyard, lined with
back-to-back houses.

Shops built into the front of a back-to-back terrace.

courtyard as clean as possible. Despite this, the level of overcrowding was such that conditions were squalid and disease was rife.

Over 40,000 back-to-backs were built in Birmingham in the first half of the 19th century, most of them in this immediate area, close to the city centre and thus within easy travelling distance to work. As the century progressed and the inhabitants became more affluent, so too did the back-to-backs evolve, becoming less basic and often having their own scullery indoors. Shops were often developed in the ground floors of street-facing properties, and often enterprising artisans set up their workshops in them. Back-to-backs were still lived in until the 1960s, when the last families were rehoused. Most of the area was flattened to make room for redevelopment, but three back-to-backs survived and have now been reopened by the National Trust to provide a fascinating insight into 19th-century city life.

Back-to-Backs open the year round, but limited opening times and admission is by timed ticket, so advance booking is advisable. There is an admission charge, free to National Trust members. For information on opening times and booking, call 0121 753 7757.

Follow Inge Street to its end and then turn right up Essex Street to reach the busy Bristol Road. Turn left along Bristol Road.

This area just south of the city centre, in an arc running from Digbeth Road on the east to Broad Street on the west, and bisected by the Bristol Road, has since the early 19th century been an area of cheap housing that was attractive to migrants into the city. As each wave of new immigrants became established and more prosperous, they moved further out from the city centre into more affluent districts, and their place was taken by the next group of newcomers. Each new community established retailing, catering and service businesses particular to their needs. Today much of this area is given over to commercial properties, but its past is still reflected in the banks and restaurants that line the Bristol Road. In the next block you pass an Indian restaurant, a Caribbean restaurant and a branch of the Bank of Cyprus.

Cross a side road (Bromsgrove Street) to reach the Wellington Hotel.

While most of the Bristol Road has been redeveloped, either between the wars or since the 1960s, some older buildings survive, and the block in front of you is a good example of these. In the 1790s a row of three-storey town houses was built as an early attempt to gentrify the Bristol Road, where good and direct communications into the city as well as out into the country to the south were seen as a draw for Birmingham's expanding middle class. As these up market homes were in the middle of a deprived area, this venture was not successful,

The Wellington Hotel, an early attempt to gentrify the Bristol Road.

and part of this block was converted in 1818 into the Wellington Hotel. An extra storey was added to provide additional accommodation and a new commercial frontage built on to the road. The Wellington, strategically placed on one of the main roads into Birmingham from the south, flourished as a hotel until the early 20th century. It was extensively rebuilt in the 1890s when a billiard room was added, and the ground floor we see today was rebuilt in the 1930s, but the upper storeys retain most of their 1890s features.

Keep ahead along Bristol Street, soon crossing Wrentham Street to reach Stratstones, showroom for Jaguar and Aston Martin. Opposite Stratstones, cross Bristol Road at pedestrian lights.

A quarter of a mile ahead of us is Birmingham's Central Mosque. It was built in 1980 to serve the city's growing Muslim population and follows the traditional design of a mosque, with a large central dome and minaret. It has a capacity for 200 worshippers. The Central Mosque was by no means the first to be built in the city: a mosque was opened in 1943 in Balsall Heath to serve the small Yemeni community there, and in 1944 the first mosque built to serve the growing Indian community was opened in Edgbaston. Migrants from Pakistan and Bangladesh started to arrive in Birmingham in significant numbers in the 1950s, concentrating initially in the areas south and east of here, and mosques were opened in Sparkbrook and surrounding districts. The City Council was well aware of the dangers of ghettoisation and began, in the 1980s, to take a more active role in promoting good relations between communities, and in putting money behind schemes to create more equal opportunities for social amenities as well as employment.

On the far side of the dual carriageway, turn right to reach St Catherine's Church.

St Catherine's Roman Catholic Church was opened in 1965, but there had been a large Catholic community, mainly Irish, in this area since the early 19th century. The first Catholic church was opened in 1786 in Broad Street, half a mile north-west of here, and such was the rate of Irish immigration into Birmingham that by 1841 the community was large enough to support a Catholic cathedral, St Chad's (see Walk 5). The Irish migrants found themselves crammed into slums, many of them in overcrowded back-to-backs, and community relations between the new migrants and the indigenous population often deteriorated into violence. The area we have just walked through was, in the mid-19th century, a police 'no-go' area, with disputes between neighbours

St Catherine's Church, Bristol Road.

Pagoda commemorating Birmingham's Chinese community.

in the crowded slums often being settled with weapons, and regular gang warfare both within and between communities.

A second wave of Irish immigration occurred after World War Two, when a labour shortage in the council workforce coincided with a lack of work in the Irish Republic. Many Irish immigrants settled here in the Digbeth–Bristol Road area of Birmingham, where there was already an established, albeit diminishing, Irish population. St Catherine's dates from this time.

Immediately after the church turn left up Irving Street and 50 yards later turn right into Bow Street. Bear right with the road, and at the top of a short slope, turn right down Exeter Street to reach the busy Holloway Head.

Chinese workers first came to Birmingham during World War One to work in the factories, and stayed on to form a small community, living in the few blocks here, around Holloway Head. The first Chinese restaurant was opened here in 1956, opposite what is now the entrance to Cleveland Tower, where a run-down shop and sauna now stand.

If you look right, down the road to Holloway Circus, you will see a grey granite tower standing in the middle of the traffic island. This is built in the style of a Chinese pagoda and commemorates the small but vibrant Chinese community that established itself in this area.

Cross the road and go up Blucher Street opposite, soon crossing Brownsea Drive.

On the right-hand corner of Brownsea Drive is Trefoil House, the headquarters of the Girl Guide Movement in Birmingham. It was opened in 1964 by Mrs W.A. Cadbury, of the Bourneville chocolate dynasty (see Walk 12).

Keep ahead to the end of Blucher Street, with the Mailbox in front of you.

Just before you reach the corner, on the right hand side of the road is the Singer Street Synagogue. The first record of Jewish immigrants into Birmingham is found in the 1767 Trade Directory, and by 1800 there was a small but well-established Jewish community in the city. Most of the immigrants came from Poland and Germany and moved into an area known as the Froggery. This was a damp, low-lying area, where the present New Street Station now stands, and the housing was among the poorest in Birmingham. Many of the first Jewish

The Singer Street synagogue.

immigrants initially worked as hawkers, street traders who plied their trade around the Bull Ring, but as they became more prosperous they established fixed businesses, particularly in the jewellery and clothing trades. The community also expanded westwards, to better quality housing around Blucher Street, Severn Street and the Holloway Head. A second synagogue (the first was in the Froggery) was built in Severn Street, just around the corner from here, in 1809.

The Jews at that time were marginalized, barred from entering public office by the Test and Corporation Acts and subject to suspicion and violence from their neighbours. The Severn Street Synagogue was wrecked by a mob in 1813, and it was not until 1827 that money could be raised for its repair. With the repeal of the Test and Corporation Acts in 1827, the Jewish community had the opportunity to more fully enter into the life of the city and cease to be marginalised. By 1851 there were a thousand Jews living in Birmingham, with 16 Jewish businesses, and Jews playing an increasingly important role in trade associations. A sign of the increasing affluence of the community was the decision to build another, grander, synagogue to replace the old one in Severn Street. Yeoville Thomason, the architect responsible for so many of Birmingham's major civic buildings, was commissioned to design the new building. Thomason came up with an elaborate Italianate building, a grandiose structure that was the first of the so-called 'cathedral synagogues' in Britain. The

The Mailbox, built into the former postal sorting office.

synagogue opened in 1855 and became the foremost synagogue in the city. Seven years later a Jewish school, also designed by Thomason, was built next to it.

In front of the Mailbox, turn right down Severn Street.

The Mailbox was originally a postal sorting office, the largest in England when it was built in 1970. Incorporated into its wall, on your left as you walk down Severn Street, is a far older building, the Athol Masonic Hall. This in turn was converted from an older building still, namely the original Severn Street Synagogue. Rebuilt in 1827 after suffering virtual destruction at the hands of a mob 14 years earlier, this synagogue remained in use until the far grander synagogue was opened just around the corner. This building then stood empty for 20 years, until in 1871 the Freemasons took it over as a meeting place. The building was extensively renovated and altered in the 1890s but then remained in use for many decades, until the GPO bought the site to construct a sorting office.

On reaching the main dual carriageway (Bristol Road) again, turn left down an access road in front of the Mailbox.

The Post Office vacated their sorting office in the mid-1990s and converted it between 1999–2001 into an elaborate complex of flats, shops and two hotels. The impressive frontage, with an elaborate sweep of steps leading up to an Italianate entrance, all dark glass and metal, is both modern and also echoes a grander architectural past. From the entrance, a long shop-lined corridor leads to escalators that in turn lead through to cafés located upon the canal side (see Walk 6).

Turn right to pass underneath the Bristol Road. Keep ahead for 100 yards along the road you enter to reach traffic lights. Turn left up Hill Street and follow the road back to Victoria Square.

Walk 9

Edgbaston: the creation of luxury suburbia

By the 19th century there had grown up in Birmingham a class of wealthy citizens, professional men, merchants and industrialists, who worked in the town but wished to live in greener, leafier surroundings. They created the demand for quality housing in a pleasant environment, but within easy commuting distance of their places of work. It was George Gough, 3rd Lord Calthorpe, who set about meeting that demand.

Sir Richard Gough had bought the Edgbaston estate in 1717. Then, it was a rural complex of fields and meadows on the outskirts of Birmingham, with a modest manor house surrounded by the humble cottages of the estate workers. Sir Richard rebuilt the manor house as Edgbaston Hall, and for the rest of the century he and his descendants lived the life of country gentlemen, acquiring the title Lord Calthorpe in 1796. It was Sir Richard's great-grandson, George, who first realised the Edgbaston estate was worth more as building land than farmland, and in 1810 he started to displace his agricultural tenants and replace them with wealthy city dwellers.

From the very outset, the policy was to attract only the wealthiest, by offering luxurious houses surrounded by small but attractive gardens, which offered privacy and exclusivity on attractive leases. Although the development of the estate, due to the vagaries of the economy, was often slow, what was created was the most exclusive suburb in Birmingham. Edgbaston is almost unique in a British city in providing a middle-class suburb that has fine houses and a low density of building, but is also less than two miles from the town centre.

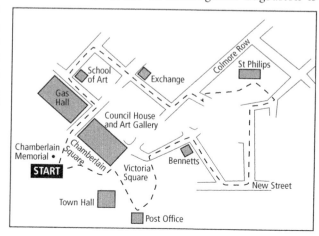

Start
This walk starts at Fiveways Station. There is a frequent train service from New Street Station.

From the station turn left and follow the dual carriageway to a busy intersection, where the Fiveways Shopping Centre is on your right.

Keep ahead to go down the subway and across the central island, entering the opposite subway to emerge on the north side of Hagley Road.

The first housing developments on the Edgbaston estate were here, at the junction of the Hagley and Harborne roads. In 1786 a handful of leases were granted for the building of town houses on previously agricultural land. Very few houses were initially built, and it was not until 1810 that the building boom really got under way. Among the earliest houses to be built were some affluent terraced houses, built here at the city end of Hagley Road in the 1820s. These were the only terraces in Edgbaston, all later developments being of detached or semi-detached properties. Those 19th-century terraces have long been swept away by the mainly post-war development we see today.

A brief detour down the side street on your right (Francis Road) brings you to the Lench's Trust Almshouses.

William Lench was one of Birmingham's wealthiest citizens during the reign of Henry VIII, owning a number of houses and plots of land across the town and surrounding countryside. In 1525 he created a trust giving the management of various of his properties over to a management committee, with the stipulation that the rents from them be used to upkeep roads and bridges in the town, and also to support charitable work among the town's poor and sick. Establishing such trusts was not an uncommon means of dispensing charity, but usually the management of trusts was given to the church, or linked in some way to religious practices such as churchmen praying for the benefactor's soul. Had Lench done the same, his trust would have shared the fate of many others and been swept away in the Reformation. But as it was set up under secular management, it survived. Over the next 150 years other citizens donated some of their properties to Lench's Trust, which is today the only surviving mediaeval charity in the city.

In the early 17th century the managers of the trust decided to build almshouses to support the 'deserving poor'. To be eligible to live in one of the almshouses the recipients had to be people 'of good character', sober and church-going, and to have been born in Birmingham. The first of the Lench's

The Plough and Harrow, a former coaching inn on the Hagley Road.

Trust almshouses was built in Digbeth, with others soon being opened across the town. The almshouses here were built in 1858, replacing earlier ones but still managed by the Lench's Trust.

Walk along Hagley Road, the road on your left, passing Tricorn House. Continue along Hagley Road to traffic lights.

On your right is the Plough and Harrow public house, built in 1852. This replaced a previous coaching inn that stood on the site. The Hagley Road was one of the main arteries into Birmingham from the west, and in the mid-18th century it had been upgraded as a turnpike road, a road maintained to a high standard by charging tolls to travellers. Stage-coaches plied the route from Birmingham to Wales, and the original inn here provided a change of horses and refreshment for travellers. The stables of that previous inn can be seen on the side of the building. The new inn was constructed in a style known as Tudor Revival, with pink sandstone dressings on top of the orange brick so associated with Birmingham.

Cross the side road (Plough and Harrow Road) and keep ahead for 100 yards to reach the Oratory.

Hagley Oratory.

With the steady increase in migrants from Ireland during the early years of the 19th century, there was a corresponding growth in Catholicism (see Walk 8). The first Roman Catholic church, St Peter's, had been opened in Broad Street in 1786. A second, St Chad's, soon to be the city's Catholic cathedral, opened in 1808 (see Walk 5). A number of other churches followed as the century progressed. In 1845 Birmingham's Catholic community was joined by a man soon to become one of the country's leading Catholic thinkers and writers, John Henry Newman.

Newman converted to Catholicism in 1845 and founded an order called the English Congregation of the Oratory of St Phillip Neri, soon known as 'Oratorians', who believed in helping people with deeds as well as prayers. Newman and his family opened a church-cum-community centre in a disused gin distillery in Alcester Street in 1849, ministering to the poor and providing food and shelter as well as spiritual comfort. In 1851 Newman bought this site in Hagley Road and commissioned the building of a religious complex here in the heart of the city.

Central to the complex is a fine church, built in a classical Italianate style in the form of a Latin cross. Newman loved classical Catholic architecture. He had no time for the starker design used by Augustus Pugin when building St Chad's Cathedral (see Walk 5), and the Oratory church was a deliberate throwback to the sumptuous churches of the Mediterranean. The church we see today was rebuilt in 1909 but preserves many of the features of Newman's original. The nave has seven bays lined with Corinthian pillars, the transepts are short and lead off a high-domed basilica and the high altar stands in a columned apse. The church is highly decorated with a riot of pink and green marble pillars, elaborate mosaics and richly decorated ceilings.

Outside the church is a cloister, on the southern side of which, facing on to Hagley Road, is Oratory House, built as a home for Newman and his family. His study and library have been preserved intact to this day. But Newman intended his Oratory to be a centre for learning as well as a church, and around the cloister are also a school hall, a refectory, and accommodation for students. Newman soon became one of Britain's leading Catholic theologians, and in 1879 he was made a Cardinal. His reputation gave the Oratory international standing, not only in religious study but also in literary and artistic pursuits. Edward Elgar lived at the Oratory while he was setting Newman's poem *The Dream of Gerontius* to music; the poet Gerald Manley Hopkins was a novice priest in the Oratory in 1867 and J.R.R. Tolkien came on retreat here for some months in 1904 (see Walk 4).

Continue along Hagley Road to the next set of traffic lights. Turn left across Hagley Road and go into Chad Road opposite. Follow the tree-lined Chad Road.

The triangle bordered by Hagley Road to the north, Harbourne Road on the south and Chad Road on the west was the first major development in Edgbaston, built in the 1850s. Chad Road was lined with fine detached houses, among the most opulent in Edgbaston, standing in large, tree-lined gardens. The houses displayed a wealth of architectural styles, many of them Georgian, but some in a style known as Greek Revival and some, with elaborate pillared frontages, distinctly Palladian. This was in part a deliberate policy, to create a measure of individuality among houses in the same road, in part the result of leases being granted to many different property developers, all of whom employed different builders and architects. Although many of the original buildings have been demolished, there are still enough fine 19th-century villas along Chad Road to convey the impression of its original grandeur.

Cross Augustus Road and keep ahead down Harborne Road. Turn first left into Westbourne Road and keep ahead.

On your right you soon come to the Botanical Gardens, founded by the 3rd Lord Calthorpe in 1831 and laid out in the grounds of a former large town house called Holly Bank. The early 19th century saw not only an increase in scientific inquiry, but also a popular upsurge in the thirst for knowledge about

Entrance to the Botanical Gardens.

the world around us. The gardens were founded to encourage the study of exotic plants, which had been brought into Britain in increasing numbers by traders and explorers ever since the 16th century. But they were also laid out as a pleasure park for the public, who could wander among bandstands and fountains while wondering at the strange plant life they were seeing. Lord Calthorpe was a devout Evangelical and a friend of William Wilberforce, who believed in encouraging educational institutions and in spreading the benefits of knowledge as widely as possible.

The gardens cover 15 acres, much of it laid out in themed beds of plants, such as alpines, herbaceous plants and so on, interspersed with glasshouses containing tropical and sub-tropical plants. The original design of the gardens was by J.C. Loudon, a leading garden planner and horticultural writer. Loudon's design still survives in large part, as does the original entrance lodge, although the latter has been considerably extended by the addition in 1986 of a glassed exhibition hall, built in a style that imitates the Terrace Glasshouses further into the gardens. The Botanical Gardens also house an aviary and are home to the National Bonsai Collection.

The Botanical Gardens are open daily from 9am until dusk or 7pm, whichever is sooner. There is an admission fee.

Follow Westbourne Road to reach a crossroads, St George's Church on your left.

St George's Church was built between 1836 and 1855, using local grey-brown sandstone from nearby Alvechurch. By this time, Edgbaston had a large population of affluent middle-class inhabitants and wanted a place of worship of its own, but one built on a grand and imposing scale. St George's originally had a nave comprised of six bays, with side aisles and a chancel, but in 1884 J.A. Chatwin was commissioned to build the even larger nave we see today. The original 1830s tall, thin lancet windows still survive, as do the buttresses.

Turn right along Church Road, passing Hallfield School on your right, to reach traffic lights.

Hallfield School is a modern private school occupying much older buildings. The main school building was a large villa, Beech Lawn, built in around 1860 and standing in extensive private grounds. The Gothic lodge was built at the same time.

Cross at the traffic lights and keep ahead.

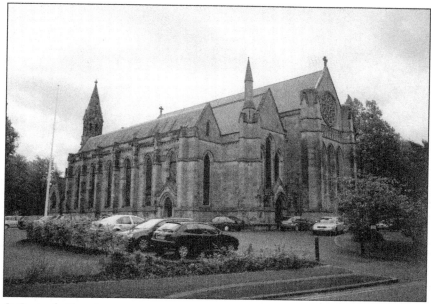

St George's Church.

Entrance to Hallfield School.

Gatehouse to the former Edgbaston Hall.

A few yards along the road, on your right, is the entrance to Edgbaston Hall, today a golf club. Sir Richard Gough bought the Edgbaston Estate in 1717 and employed Warwick architect Francis Smith to rebuild the existing mediaeval hall as a suitable home for him. Smith created a three-storey brick mansion, with a pillared porch leading into an entrance hall, dominated by a magnificent sweeping staircase. The hall contained a library, snooker room and several reception rooms; all the trappings of a gentleman's country house. The hall was extensively redesigned in 1850, at which time the gatehouse lodge was built. Today the hall is the clubhouse of the golf club.

In the 1770s Edgbaston Hall was bought by Dr William Withering, who was a part of a select group known as the Lunar Society, one of a number of scientific societies that grew up in the industrial cities of Victorian England. The Lunar Society was not a formal society so much as a group of like-minded individuals who had a common interest in advancing scientific knowledge, and who met at intervals to discuss matters of interest to them. Among the members were practical industrialists such as Matthew Boulton (a patient of Dr Withering's), James Watt, and Josiah Wedgewood (of pottery fame). There were also experimenters and thinkers who were interested in knowledge for its own sake. Among this latter group were men such as James Keir, an amateur chemist, Thomas Day, an educational reformer, and Dr Withering himself, another chemist whose work on botany (especially his discovery of the medicinal uses of foxgloves) became famous. The Lunar Society met at the homes of its members, and Edgbaston Hall often hosted their meetings. Since many of the Society's members had long distances to travel for evening meetings, nights well-lit by a full moon were often favoured, hence the name 'Lunar Society.'

It was the activities of another member of the Lunar Society, Joseph Priestley, that almost led to the destruction of Edgbaston Hall in 1791. Priestley was a Unitarian minister and political radical who hosted a meeting at the Dadley Hotel in central Birmingham to praise the activities of the French Revolution, by then in its third year and becoming increasingly violent and radical. This meeting provoked a demonstration by anti-French/anti-liberal citizens. The demonstrators, fuelled by drink, soon got out of hand: the Dadley Hotel was attacked, rioters then marched to Moor Street to burn Priestley's chapel (see Walk 5) and then proceeded out to Sparkbrook to burn his house. Over the next four days and nights the rioting spread across the city, with the homes of wealthy families, especially those associated with either Priestley in particular or with Liberalism in general, being targeted and in several cases totally destroyed. Edgbaston Hall was attacked, fortunately when Wittering and his family were not at home, and was only saved from destruction by its well-stocked wine cellar, which distracted the rioters until the military arrived from Warwick Barracks to restore order.

St Bartholemew's, or Edgbaston Old Church, dates from 1279.

Continue for a few yards more, to reach the church on your right.

This is St Bartholomew's Church, or Edgbaston Old Church as it is often known, one of the oldest churches within the modern city of Birmingham. The suffix 'ton' gives away Edgbaston's Anglo-Saxon origins, and there was a small farming community here in around AD700, at the time that Beorma was establishing his new village of Birmingham two miles to the east. It is unknown whether there was a church here in Saxon times: the first reference to St Bartholomew's is in 1279 and it is likely that, as Edgbaston expanded in the centuries after the Norman Conquest, a church was built to serve the community. The original church was a simple structure, primarily a long nave and chancel. An aisle was added on the northern side in around 1500, and the tower was built shortly afterwards.

St Bartholomew's was severely damaged during the Civil War. When that conflict started, Birmingham supported the Parliamentarian cause. Its gun-makers supplied weaponry for Parliament's army, its merchants contributed money to Parliament's coffers, and many of its churchmen, sympathetic to Puritanism, preached against the High Church Anglicanism favoured by the king. Birmingham was to pay heavily for its stance, for on Easter Monday 1643 a Royalist army, led by the king's nephew Prince Rupert, attacked the town. Birmingham, with no formal defences, could put up little resistance, and the Royalists occupied the city. Rupert made little attempt to control his troops, who indulged in an orgy of rape and pillaging. Many buildings, St Bartholomew's included, were sacked and damaged.

The church was restored after the Civil War to its former glory, but in Victorian times the building was substantially altered. Between 1844–50 a south aisle, a new porch and a vestry were added, windows were altered and walls raised. Further alterations followed in 1885, when a chapel and arcade were added, a new chancel was built and the nave walls further raised. The church we see today is largely the Victorian reconstruction, although much of the original mediaeval brickwork can still be seen in the outer wall facing the road.

The interior of the church is mainly Victorian, but contains some interesting monuments from earlier times. Several owners of Edgbaston Hall, who have played a significant part in our story of Edgbaston, are commemorated here, including Sir Richard Gough, his great-grandson George, Lord Calthorpe, and Dr William Withering.

Continue past the church for a few yards to reach a roundabout. Turn left, passing Priory School on the opposite side of the road.

Priory School.

Until the end of the 18th century education was only at a rudimentary level. Many schools were run as charities, the majority operated by the Church of England. Qualified teachers were a rarity and very often it was left to men and women with only a basic education themselves to drum into their pupils the basics of literacy and arithmetic. In 1838 only one in five children in Birmingham received any type of formal education and these pupils were predominantly boys: girls were expected to acquire the skills necessary to run a household from their mothers, and this was all the education it was deemed they needed.

Priory School was founded as a private school to educate the children of Edgbaston's new middle classes. It was not a charitable institution but charged fees for its pupils, and was thus able to afford better qualified teachers. Originally the number of pupils it took was so small that the school was housed in a villa, originally built in 1829 as a home for a wealthy citizen. As numbers of pupils expanded, they outgrew the original building and a larger block was added in 1879, although it was designed to be in keeping with the original school building.

Turn left into Ampton Road and keep ahead to cross Arthur Road. Keep ahead along Ampton Road.

The Walker Memorial Hall, built as a parish school in 1847.

On your left is the Walker Memorial Hall, originally a school. Unlike Priory School, this was a parish school, funded by the parish of Edgbaston to provide basic education to the boys of the neighbourhood. The simple building, housing two classrooms, was purpose built in 1847, in a mock-Tudor style. No. 47 Ampton Road was built slightly later as the schoolmaster's house.

At the end of Ampton Road turn right into Carpenter Road. Follow this road down to a crossroads and turn left into Wheeleys Road.

Climb Wheeleys Road, passing the ends of several private closes and mews. At the next crossroads turn left into St James Road.

On your left, just after turning the corner into St James Road, is the Round House. This curious building was built in 1818 as a garden house, a very elaborate gazebo standing in the grounds of one of the large private houses that lined St James Road. The house was sold off to developers in the 1820s who built several smaller properties in its grounds. In 1827 the Round House was itself turned into a dwelling by adding an extra block on to each side.

Keep ahead along St James Road and then turn right into George Road. Follow George Road to its junction with the main road. Turn right along the road back to Fiveways Station.

Walk 10

A walk though the heart of Victorian Birmingham

The Industrial Revolution had resulted in Birmingham becoming the foremost manufacturing town in Britain, and the large-scale political reforms of the 1830s cemented Birmingham's position as a great municipality. But it was in the 1870s and 1880s that Birmingham blossomed to become the epitome of late Victorian England. The influence of two men, both visionaries in their different ways, was behind this transformation. Joseph Chamberlain was Lord Mayor of Birmingham, and set about rebuilding the municipal buildings in the town centre with the grandeur the status of England's second city required. John Ruskin was an influential thinker and writer, who believed that industrial technology posed a danger to both the environment and society. He believed that urban man deserved to live in pleasant surroundings, and that buildings should be aesthetic as well as functional. Ruskin's ideas inspired many of the architects who built Chamberlain's Birmingham. This walk takes us through the city that was created in that era.

Start

This walk starts at the Chamberlain Memorial Fountain, in front of the library steps in Chamberlain Square.

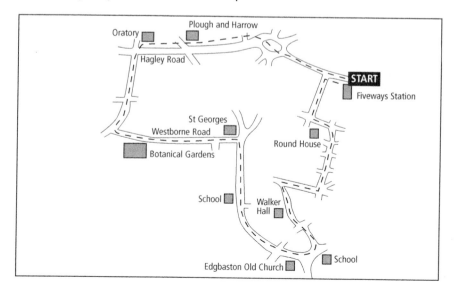

Although Joseph Chamberlain is always associated with Birmingham, he was actually born in London In 1854, aged 18, Chamberlain moved to Birmingham to work in his uncle's company, Nettlefold & Chamberlain, later to become the country's largest screw-making company and later still to become GKN. Joseph entered politics in 1869 as Liberal councillor for St Pails ward. Four years later, in 1873, he was elected Lord Mayor of Birmingham.

Since it was formed in 1851 Birmingham Council had made significant reforms to the provision of social services to the city, but Chamberlain took that work to a whole new level. He reformed the city's finances, with strategic long-term planning and careful but massive borrowing. He took over the gas services, providing cheaper heat and light to households while using the profits for public investment. He brought provision of water to the city under the control of the council, regularising supply while building for the future with the ambitious Elan Valley reservoir scheme. He used this new financial stability to undertake ambitious programmes of slum clearance, and improved amenities such as roads, schools and libraries. He also set about rebuilding the public buildings in central Birmingham to provide a municipal heart worthy of the nation's second city.

Chamberlain was mayor for only three years, entering Parliament as a Liberal MP in 1876. He served under Gladstone as President of the Board of Trade from 1880–85, but his belief in partial Home Rule for Ireland was at odds with his party and he resigned from the Liberals. He joined the Conservatives and was

Medallion of Joseph Chamberlain on the Chamberlain Fountain.

The Birmingham Museum and Art Gallery.

Colonial Secretary for Lord Salisbury from 1895 until 1902. During those years he sponsored such social reforms as the Workers Compensation Act, but his energies were largely engaged with the colonies and especially with the Boer War (see Walk 7). Chamberlain left politics after a paralysing stroke in 1906 and died in 1914. His sons, Austin and Neville, both became MPs and Neville later became Prime Minister.

Although Joseph Chamberlain was one of the dominant figures in late Victorian politics, in Birmingham he is still primarily remembered for his work as Lord Mayor.

Stand in front of the Chamberlain Memorial Fountain.

The Chamberlain Memorial Fountain was designed by architect John Henry Chamberlain, a close associate of but no relation to Joseph Chamberlain, and unveiled in 1880. J.H. Chamberlain was strongly influenced by the great Liberal thinker John Ruskin, and the fountain, seeming to combine the industrial with the pastoral, reflects this influence. At the top of the fountain is a medallion head of Joseph Chamberlain, which was sculpted by Thomas Woolner.

With your back to the Chamberlain Memorial, turn and face the Museum and Art Gallery. The main Art Gallery building, with the

The clock tower of 'Big Brum' and the Chamberlain Fountain.

clock tower, is to the right, with an extension (called the Gas Hall) on the left side of the pedestrianised Edmund Street and connected to the main building by a bridge.

The Museum and Art Gallery has been built on to the back of the Council House. Creating a new Council House of sufficient grandeur to epitomise the new Birmingham was the major building project of Joseph Chamberlain's era. The initial concept envisaged Law Courts on the back of the Council House that would be entered from here, Chamberlain Square. These plans were soon altered, and the decision to build the Law Courts elsewhere left the back of the site empty (see Walk 5).

At much the same time, 1880, local industrialists the Tangye brothers gave £10,000 to the city to buy works of art, on condition a new Art Gallery was built to house the collection. The back of the Council House was the obvious site for this, but finance now became an issue. However, a deal was done with the embarrassingly profitable municipal Gas Department, whereby those profits would be used to build an Art Gallery at first-floor level, while the Gas Department would occupy offices below.

Work started on the Museum and Art Gallery in 1881, to designs by H.R. Yeoville Thomason, another architect inspired by the ideas of John Ruskin. The imposing main façade looks out on to Chamberlain Square, with the tall clock

The Art Gallery is connected to the former Gas Building by a bridge.

tower, known as 'Big Brum', standing to one side of the building. The galleries were first opened to the public in 1885 and work on the building finally finished in1890. By 1908, however, the collection had outgrown the space available, and an extension was built on the other side of Edmund Street, linked to the main gallery by a bridge at first-floor level. Today this extension is known as the Gas Hall, commemorating its financial origins.

The main entrance to the Museum and Art Gallery faces Chamberlain Square. Inside a marble staircase leads up to the galleries, which house an extensive collection. The Industrial Gallery commemorates Victorian glass and ironwork, and there is an impressive collection of paintings and other works by the Pre-Raphaelite Brotherhood, of whom more later. The Edwardian tea-rooms are worth a visit on their own.

Open Mon –Sat 10am–5pm (10.30am on Fridays), 12.30pm–5pm on Sundays.

Walk towards the museum and bear left to pass under the bridge that links the Art Gallery proper with the Gas Hall extension.

Birmingham had been lit by gas since the early 19th century and by 1870 was supplied exclusively by the Birmingham & Staffordshire Gas Light Co. (See Walk 6.) In 1875, at Joseph Chamberlain's instigation, the Birmingham Corporation took over the company, partly so that its monopoly could be controlled by elected officials, and partly so that its huge profits could be used to fund municipal redevelopment. The new Gas Department was highly successful, making huge profits, and within 10 years was supplying gas to 600,000 private homes as well as 10,000 street lights (ironically, so successful was the supply of gas by the corporation that Birmingham was slow to take up electric lighting, a new-fangled device not seen as necessary).

Walk along the pedestrianised roadway, past the ramp leading to an underground car park and keep ahead to reach Margaret Street.

Note as you pass a short stretch of tramline set into the bricks of the roadway. The first horse-drawn tram went into operation in Birmingham in 1872, connecting Colmore Row (the next street to here) with the suburb of Hockley. A spider's web of tramways rapidly spread out from the city centre, with firstly horse-drawn, then steam-driven and finally, after 1890, electric-powered trams running alongside them. Fares were initially one penny anywhere within the network. The last electric trams disappeared from Birmingham's streets in the 1950s, replaced by buses. A tramway was reintroduced in 1997, connecting the city centre with the northern suburbs.

All that remains of Birmingham's original tramlines.

Turn left along Margaret Street, passing the Birmingham School of Art on your right.

Manufacturing in Birmingham always had a strong reliance upon skilled artisans, and this in turn enabled the Arts and Crafts Movement started by William Morris to gain considerable influence in the town. This movement was dedicated to promoting and maintaining artisan skills under threat in an age of mass industrial production and was a practical application of John Ruskin's theories. In 1885, the same year that the Art Gallery was completed, the Birmingham Institute of Art & Design (later the School of Art) was also opened. This was the first school devoted to the teaching of art opened anywhere in England.

The School of Art was the last great project by architect J.H. Chamberlain, who with his partner William Martin created many of the great municipal monuments of late Victorian Birmingham. Chamberlain, having designed the School of Art, died in 1883, and it was completed by Martin. A large part of the cost of the project was borne by the Tangye brothers, who had funded the Art Gallery. The school is built of red terracotta brick in an ornately decorated Gothic style. The gables in the main part of the building were designed to ensure natural light came into the top floor studios all day long.

Open 9am–5pm, Monday to Friday.

Turn right into Cornwell Street, passing between the School of Art on your right and the equally imposing Birmingham & Midland Institute on your left.

The Birmingham & Midland Institute was built as the Birmingham Library, a private members library, in 1889–90. It is a simplified companion piece to the School of Art. The institute moved into the building in 1973. At that time it was a further education college for mechanics.

At the next crossroads turn right into Newhall Street. Continue along Newhall Street, to cross over Edmund Street.

On your left, at No. 19 Newhall Street on the corner of Edmund Street, is the splendid Exchange Building, built out of the highly ornate terracotta that was typical of Victorian Birmingham. This building, designed by Frederick Martin (son of William) of Martin & Chamberlain, was built to house the telephone exchange for the Bell Edison Telephone Company, and was opened in 1896. Today the Exchange Building houses suites of modern offices.

Follow Newhall Street until you reach Colmore Row and turn left. Continue along Colmore Row to reach St Phillip's Cathedral. Just before St Phillip's, turn right into Temple Row West for 30 yards to reach the Joint Stock Company building.

For Birmingham to flourish as a manufacturing town, it was not only necessary for entrepreneurs to recognise and build new business ventures. These businesses also needed finance from venture capitalists who were prepared to risk investing in cutting-edge technology. The Joint Stock Company building was the headquarters for such a group of capitalists, private financiers and bankers who lent the money that helped fuel Birmingham's rise to greatness.

Return to the corner of Temple Row West and then enter the churchyard. Follow the path to the main door of St Phillip's Cathedral.

The original settlement of Birmingham was around the parish church of St Martin's, near today's Bullring, sheltering below the ridge that marked the town's northern boundary. You are now standing on the summit of that ridge, with the earliest town down the slope to your right, while down the slope to your left were the orchards and open fields of the Newhall Estate (see Walk 7). In the 17th century Birmingham grew dramatically, spreading northwards up the slope of the ridge. To serve the ever-increasing population it was decided to build a second parish church here, at the highest point of the town.

Land was donated by two local landowners, William Ing and Penelope Phillips, and work started upon St Phillip's Church in 1708 (its name owes nothing to any association between St Phillip and Birmingham, rather being named after the donor of the land). The architect chosen to design it was Thomas Archer, a pupil of Christopher Wren, who had worked with his master designing a number of new churches built in London to replace those lost in the Great Fire. Archer was a local man, his family owning the large estate of Umberslade Hall, 12 miles south of the city. An enigmatic monument to Archer stands in the grounds at Umberslade, clearly visible to motorists just as they join the M40 going south. Like many young gentlemen of his day, Archer had completed his education by taking a Grand Tour of Europe, where the architecture of classical Italy made a great impression upon him.

St Phillip's was built in a simplified form of the elaborate Italian architecture, in a style known as the English Baroque. It was designed as a rectangle with seven bays, divided by Doric pillars, with a tower at one end and an apse at the other. The tower, with its concave walls, octagonal dome housing a domed

St Phillip's Cathedral.

lantern and fluted piers is one of the finest examples of the English Baroque in existence. The church was built for a cost of £5,000, a significant sum of money at the time, and was consecrated in 1715.

By the end of the 19th century, coinciding with the era of epic municipal building in Birmingham, congregations at St Phillip's had grown substantially. The elevation of St Phillip's to cathedral status also looked likely, and so it was decided to enlarge the church. Archer's original small apse was replaced in 1883–84 by a new chancel designed by J.A. Chatwin. Additional columns were placed in the choir and an organ installed. Most significantly, money was given by Emma Villiers-Wilkes, heiress to a local wire manufacturing company, for the installation of three new windows at the east end of the church. These were created by the great Pre-Raphaelite artist Edward Burne-Jones, as was a fourth window at the west end. These magnificent windows were one of St Phillip's greatest gems, and among the finest stained glass of the Pre-Raphaelite movement.

In 1905 St Phillip's became a cathedral, when the Diocese of Birmingham was created. On 7 November 1940, during German bombing raids, the cathedral was hit and set on fire. Fortunately the Burne-Jones windows had already been removed for safety to a mineshaft in Wales. After the war the cathedral was faithfully restored to the condition we see it in today. The windows, however, were never reinstalled, and today can be been in the city's art gallery.

Open at all reasonable times.

After visiting St Phillip's, turn left out of the doors and pass along the southern side of the cathedral, the building on your left hand. Halfway along the side of the cathedral, take the path leading to the right, passing a needle-like obelisk.

This obelisk is a memorial to Colonel Burnaby, who served in the English army and died in an incident at Khiva during the Sudan campaign of 1875. The monument was raised in 1885 and both dates are commemorated on it.

On reaching the road at the far end, turn right and walk with the railings of St Phillip's Churchyard on your right until opposite the Louis Vuitton store. Turn left beside the store and walk down Temple Street.

Temple Street was cut in the early 18th century to connect New Street with the new building development on the top of the ridge being carried out by William Ing and Elizabeth Phillips. On the right as you walk down Temple Street, at No. 8, is the Birmingham Law Society. This building started life in 1858 as a Temperance Hall, housing offices and a library. In 19th-century Birmingham, as in all big cities, alcohol abuse was an increasing problem among a working class whose daily lives were often desperately hard and bleak. Temperance societies, dedicated to exposing and opposing the evils of drink, were started as a middle-class reaction to the social ills caused by alcohol.

At the bottom of the hill turn right along the pedestrianised New Street for 100 yards, then turn right again and walk up Bennetts Hill.

Look out for No. 12, on your left. This was the birthplace of Edward Burne-Jones, Birmingham's greatest artist and most famous of the Pre-Raphaelite painters.

The original Pre-Raphaelite Brotherhood was a group of young artists heavily influenced by the writings of John Ruskin, who rejected the grandiose and sentimental paintings that dominated early Victorian England and aimed to return to the Classical style that had reached its peak with the work of Raphael. Their style is characterised by strong, bright colour and an almost photographic attention to detail. The brotherhood was latterly joined by two men who were to become its leading protagonists, Edward Burne-Jones and William Morris.

Edward Burne-Jones, born in 1833, went to Oxford University, where he met William Morris. Both men intended to enter the church, but instead they encountered the writings of John Ruskin, with his ideas about the moral and uplifting nature of art. They turned their fervour and idealism to art, Burne-Jones to painting, William Morris founding the Arts and Crafts movement. Both returned to Birmingham after leaving Oxford. Morris's beliefs inspired several of the architects behind Birmingham's renaissance, while Burne-Jones undertook some of his best work in Birmingham, notably the great stained-glass windows in St Phillip's. These, together with a number of his paintings, can be seen in the Museum and Art Gallery.

Continue up Bennetts Hill to the first crossroads.

At the top of the street, on the left-hand corner, stands Bennetts Bank. Like the Joint Stock Co., Bennetts Bank grew out of the need to finance Birmingham's entrepreneurs. But it was not enough that the bank was present in the city, it needed a prestigious building that reflected both the importance and soundness of the institution and also fitted into the grandeur of Birmingham's new municipal heart. Bennetts was first built in 1869 and enlarged in 1890. The windows are separated by Corinthian pillars, while the corner entrance is a high

The grandiose Midland Bank building.

domed porch, supported by two Doric pillars. Much of the banking hall inside is original, with a highly decorated ceiling supported by further Doric pillars.

Bennetts is open during normal banking hours.

Facing Bennetts is the Midland Bank. It too needed an imposing building, commensurate both with its own and the city's status, and it has been designed to resemble a Greek temple.

Turn left along Waterloo Street.

Until well into the 19th century this part of Birmingham remained fields and orchards, part of the Ing Estate sandwiched between the old town (which stopped at New Street) and the new developments to the east (around St Phillip's and Temple Row). From 1823 onwards a new road was built, called Waterloo Street to commemorate the famous victory over Napoleon eight years earlier, and a mixture of fashionable houses, banks and high-class shops gradually developed along it. The grandeur of these homes, built for Birmingham's social elite, such as Aspley House on the right, can still be seen.

By the beginning of the 20th century the area of Bennetts Hill was firmly established as Birmingham's banking heart, and many of the buildings in Waterloo Street were taken over by banks or finance houses.

The General Post Office, built in the style of a French chateau.

At the end of Waterloo Street, with iron railings in front of you, turn left down steps. The cascade of Victoria Square is behind the railings to your right. At the bottom of the steps turn right for a few yards to reach the Post Office building on your left.

The General Post Office building was opened in 1891 and housed Birmingham's Head Post Office until the 1970s, when it became the head office of the TSB bank. It was built in the style of a French Renaissance chateau, with a wealth of Corinthian pillars, stone urns and domed attics. In front of the building is a sculpture called *Iron: Man* by Anthony Gormley, depicting a human figure enclosed in beams and referring to the city's industrial heritage.

With the Post Office at your back, climb the steps into Victoria Square, to reach the front of the Council House.

Although Victoria Square is now the central civic square in Birmingham, it began life as a humble junction of roads on the edge of the expanding town. The shape of the square was defined when the Town Hall was built on the west in 1832, the Council House built to the north in 1870–74 and the General Post Office to the south in 1891.

In 1991 the square was totally redesigned, employing the work of sculptor Dhruva Mistry. A north-south axis of steps descends from the portico of the

Victoria Square, with steps and fountains leading up to the Council House.

Council House. The steps flank two ornamental pools with water flowing between them, the top pool adorned with a statue of a large female nude called *The River*, and the bottom one with a fountain faced by two smaller figures representing youth. Two sphinx-like guardians flank the bottom pool, while two slender pillars flank the upper pool. The whole effect is dramatic and exotic, and quite stunning.

Pause in front of the Council House.

The Council House was planned to be Birmingham's principal municipal

building. Although the site had been bought in 1853, shortage of funds and concerns about the economic future left it undeveloped for 20 years. New life was breathed into the project when Joseph Chamberlain

The Council House, opened in 1879.

Statue to Queen Victoria in
Victoria Square.

became Mayor in 1873. He saw the new Council House as central to the redevelopment of Birmingham's city centre and a monument to the city's reinvigoration. Designs had already been submitted by H.R. Yeoville Thomason, but he was now persuaded to radically alter them, making the building far grander and more flamboyant. It was insisted that the design blended harmoniously with the adjacent Town Hall. The Council House was built in a Renaissance style, with a central dome and a domed arch above a columned portico. On the arch is a sculpture by Lockwood, Bowton & Sons, depicting the industrialists of Birmingham being rewarded by Britannia.

The foundation stone was laid in June 1874 by Joseph Chamberlain, and the building was formally opened in October 1879, although the council had actually been meeting in it for a year by then. As we have seen, the original plans were for Law Courts to be built on the rear of the building, but the Museum and Art Gallery was built there instead.

Turn left towards the Town Hall.

On your left is a statue to Queen Victoria, which was unveiled in 1901 and gave the square its name. This statue is a copy of one created by Thomas Brock, which stands in the Shire Hall, Worcester, and was made at the insistence of a major patron of the development of Victoria Square, Birmingham solicitor W.H. Barber. The original statue was of white marble, but it was recast in bronze in 1951.

There are more statues to Queen Victoria than to any other British monarch, and no town of any size seems to be without one. Most were created in the latter half of Victoria's reign, and reflect not only the general affection the queen was held in, but also pride in the country she ruled and the era to which she gave her name.

The Town Hall.

Pause in front of the Town Hall.

By the start of the 19th century, Birmingham was growing fast, but there was no centralised planning or control of its development. The town was still run by a body called the Street Commissioners, a non-elected body created by Act of Parliament. In 1828 the Street Commissioners were given permission to build a Town Hall, which could accommodate 3,000 people. The building of a dedicated Town Hall was seen as an essential step towards public accountability, where not only could the Commissioners conduct business, but there was ample room for all ratepayers to attend public meetings and contribute to the Commissioners' deliberations. The hall would have a dual function by providing a venue for musical festivals as well.

In 1830 a competition was held for the design of the new Town Hall. Out of over 70 entries, that submitted by architects Edward Welch and Joseph Hansom (who went on to invent the Hansom cab) was finally selected. The radical politics of the pair may have helped them win. This was a time of great political unrest. Thomas Attwood, who was chairman of the Street Commissioners and had a major say in the selection of the Town Hall design, was also a leading light in the Birmingham Political Union. He was organising mass campaigns in favour of the Reform Bill, a campaign supported by Hansom and Welch (see Walk 7).

The design for the Town Hall was revolutionary. It was modelled on the Temple of Castor and Pollux in the Forum at Rome, and was the first substantial building in the Roman Revival style later to be so popular in 19th-century Britain. Work started in 1832, building a hall 12 bays long by eight wide, each bay flanked with Corinthian columns and the whole hall standing on a huge raised podium. The building was of brick, faced with marble from the Isle of Anglesey to give it its majestic and monumental appearance.

The project ran into difficulties almost immediately. The original budget was £17,000, but by the time work was completed in 1834 it had cost over £25,000, bankrupting Hansom in the process. Almost immediately it was realised that the hall had insufficient room to accommodate an orchestra. In 1849 the opening of new roads to the north and west of the Hall enabled it to be extended, adding two more bays to its length. Later alterations were to follow: the entrance was much enlarged in the 1880s, the interior was redesigned in 1926 and a gallery was added with a richly decorated ceiling.

The Town Hall ceased to be used for municipal business in 1874, when the Council House was opened next door, but it continued to be used for cultural functions. The Birmingham Triennial Musical Festival was held from 1834 until its demise in 1917 and it was home to the Birmingham Symphony Orchestra from 1918 until 1991.

Charles Dickens gave readings here to packed houses, and political rallies were held throughout its history (Lloyd George provoked a near-riot by speaking against the Boer War in 1900 and had to escape disguised as a policeman). The hall finally closed for refurbishment in 1996 and reopened in 2007.

At the time it was built there was much criticism of the Town Hall. It was seen by many as too huge and grandiloquent a building for a provincial town, 'an ocean liner anchored in a fishing village' being one description of it. Nevertheless, Thomas Attwood and the Street Commissioners had a vision of what Birmingham would become and built accordingly, and in doing so laid the foundation for the wonderful municipal architecture that was to follow.

Turn right between the Town Hall and the Council House to return to Chamberlain Square.

Walk 11

Brains and Architecture: a walk through the University Quarter

In 1880 a science college, Mason College, was founded and housed in old Gothic buildings in Edmund Street in the city centre. In 1898 it became Mason University College, receiving its charter as a university two years later. Joseph Chamberlain, who was its first Chancellor, had been largely instrumental in obtaining University status for the college. Chamberlain had always been an ardent advocate of further education and supported many developments whose aim was to increase the knowledge base of Birmingham (see Walks 7 and 10). 'Brains not architecture' was how he described his vision of the new university in the course of conversation with Andrew Carnegie, the American steel magnate and philanthropist. Carnegie's view was, perhaps fortunately, less utilitarian than Chamberlain's. He donated £50,000 to the new university in order to establish a 'first-class modern scientific college', but on condition that new and prestigious buildings were raised.

That same year, 1900, Lord Calthorpe, owner of the Edgbaston Estate, three miles south of the city centre, gave 25 acres of his estate to provide a home for a purpose-built university (see Walk 9). Architects Aston Webb and Ingress Bell, who had just built the highly acclaimed Victoria Law Courts in Corporation Street (see Walk 5), were chosen to design the new campus. The campus they built was greatly influenced by a style known as 'Beaux Arts', popular with many American universities in the 1890s, and was the first formally planned English university. It was officially opened in 1909 by King Edward VII.

The inter-war expansion of the university campus remained in keeping with

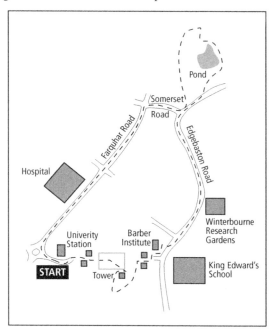

Webb and Bell's original design concept. In 1945 it was decided to bring the rest of the university's faculties, at that time scattered across the city centre, on to the Edgbaston campus. Various plans for extension were considered until finally, in 1957, the commission was awarded to Sir Hugh Casson and Neville Conder, the foremost designers of university campuses in the country.

Start

This walk starts from University Station. There is a frequent train service from New Street station to University Station.

From University Station turn left, cross the canal and then cross the road , passing to the right of the statue. Continue down the slope, passing between the Learning Centre on the left and the Computer Science block on the right.

The first part of this walk takes us back in time, through the various stages of the university's development. The blocks you are walking through were part of the post-war expansion of the university on to newly-acquired land to the north and west of the original campus.

Keep ahead to reach a road. Keep ahead to cross the Ring Road and carry on.

Birmingham University.

Cross the forecourt and pass through the arch beside the Staff House to enter University Square. Keep ahead across the square, but pause in the middle to look around you.

The grassy quadrangle of University Square was central to Casson and Conder's concept of Birmingham University. It was created in the 1950s, just to the north of the original university complex. With the main administrative buildings located around it, the square provided a tranquil heart to the university.

To the north (your left as you walk across the square) is the library building. Constructed in 1957–60 in a Classical style, it is five storeys high, with piers of red brick that suggest Classical pilasters and with a recessed entrance beneath a heavy cornice. A special wing was created in the library to house the political papers, diaries and correspondence of Joseph Chamberlain and his half-brother, the Prime Minister Neville Chamberlain. The collection was later enhanced by the addition of the papers of another Prime Minister, Anthony Eden, MP for nearby Warwick and Leamington. In front of the library is a statue by Barbara Hepworth, sculpted in 1970 as part of her 'Family of Man' series and called *Ancestor*.

To the east (in front of you) are the Poynting and Watson Buildings, in the same red brick as the library, housing the mathematics and physics departments.

The Great Hall and the Chamberlain Tower.

Behind you (where you entered the square) is the University Centre and connected Staff House, designed by Neville Conder and built in 1958–62, but far more modern in appearance than the Classical buildings that surround the square.

Turn right at the end of University Square.

Dominating University Square, and indeed the whole university, is the tower on the southern (right-hand) side of the square. This tower is part of the original 1909 university designed by Webb and Bell. Named Chamberlain Tower after the university's founder, it is a free-standing clock tower, modelled upon an Italian campanile or bell tower and built in the red brick that is so strongly associated with the municipal buildings of Victorian Birmingham. At the time the university was being designed, Joseph Chamberlain was holidaying in Italy and was greatly impressed by the Torre del Mangia, the campanile that dominates Sienna. He thought that such a tower would provide a suitably dramatic centrepiece to the new university, providing, in the words of the *Birmingham Daily Post*, an 'intellectual beacon of the Midlands'. Architects Webb and Bell created the Chamberlain Tower in the style of the Torre del Mangia.

Enter Chancellor's Court.

Chancellor's Court was the original centre of the university, designed by Webb and Bell at the start of the 20th century. At first glance the court has a superficial resemblance to an Oxbridge quadrangle, but on closer inspection it can be seen that both the ground plan and the style of the surrounding buildings is different. This was a deliberate act on the part of architects Webb and Bell to give a

Chamberlain Tower, modelled on the Torre de Mangia in Sienna.

153

The Great Hall.

distinctive look for the first English university devoted primarily to the study of science. The plan enabled Birmingham University to combine echoes of Oxbridge with a modern look in keeping with the city's vision of itself.

As you enter from this side, Chancellor's Court is dominated by the Great Hall, facing you on the south side of the court. It has a square, three-storey entrance pavilion topped by a dome and a lantern. At each corner are square, domed turrets, and a great arched, mullioned window dominates the façade. Along the front of the building is a frieze, made out of ceramic by artist Robert Anning, which depicts the goddess Learning handing a wreath of scholarship to a kneeling man in academic dress who represents the university.

Inside the building is the hall itself, 150 feet by 75 feet, with a ribbed barrel-vaulted ceiling, a gallery and vaulted side passages on the ground and first floors. The hall is dominated by a stained-glass window, celebrating major benefactors of the university.

To either side of the Great Hall, and part of the same building, are two-storey teaching blocks, also flanked with round towers. On the ground floor are lecture theatres, with libraries and offices above.

Cross the court to the front of the Great Hall. Go left along the front of the building and at the end follow the curved walk around, to turn right through bollards to the left of the Physics West building.

You are now walking forwards in time again, through 1950s buildings contemporary with University Square.

Keep ahead, through a parking area, along a bush-lined walkway, and across a bridge over an access road. At the far end of the bridge

The statue of George I originally stood in Dublin.

turn left down to the gatekeeper's booth. Cross the entrance road and keep ahead, passing the statue of George I on your right, to the front of the Barber Institute on your left.

The statue of King George I was commissioned by the city of Dublin in 1717. This was a display of loyalty to the crown in the face of unrest from Catholic supporters of James Stuart, the 'Young Pretender' (son of the exiled James II), who had inspired an unsuccessful revolt against George I two years previously. The statue is attributed to the Dutch sculptor John van Nost the Elder, although it was probably executed by his assistants after his death, and it was unveiled in Dublin in 1722. It was bought in 1937 by Thomas Bodkin, first director of the Barber Institute, and brought to its present location.

The Barber Institute of Fine Arts is the legacy of Lady Barber. She and her husband had been long-standing patrons of the university and, shortly before her death in 1933, Lady Barber offered to fund a building dedicated to music and visual arts. Robert Atkinson, an architect noted also as a connoisseur of paintings, was chosen to design the building. While still in the planning stage, Thomas Bodkin was appointed as the institute's first director, and he decided to give more space to the arts and less to music. Atkinson accordingly modified his initial plans, and today the institute consists of a central music auditorium

The Barber Institute.

surrounded by libraries, with a sequence of art galleries on the floor above. Atkinson, a student of modern architecture, based his designs for the Barber Institute on the Boymans Museum in Rotterdam, itself strongly influenced by Scandinavian classicism.

The Barber Institute houses a permanent collection of paintings, sculptures, coins and manuscripts and hosts regular concerts and lectures.

With your back to the Barber Institute, walk ahead to reach the road. Turn right for a few yards.

To your right is the Guild of Students building, surely one of the most magnificent student union buildings of any university. It was built in 1930 and designed to be in keeping with the original Casson and Conder buildings around Chancellor's Court. It is built on a E-plan, with three large gables facing on to the road and with mock Ionic pillars on the rear face. It is made of brown brick, with the arches picked out in red brick and with stone facings.

Retrace your steps and look across the road.

On the opposite side of the road is the King Edward Grammar School. King Edward VI was a keen educationalist, and endowed many schools during his short reign, including a grammar school in Birmingham. The Guild of the Holy Cross, located on present-day New Street, had been closed during the Reformation by Henry VIII, and its lands and especially its Guild Hall were appropriated by Edward in 1552 to form the basis of his new school. Attendance was strictly limited to boys from Anglican families, wealthy for the most part, although some scholarships were available to

Entrance to King Edward Grammar School.

157

support boys from poorer homes. The original curriculum was limited, with a heavy concentration, as the name ' grammar school' suggests, upon the teaching of Latin, although associated areas, such as literature and philosophy, were also studied. The aim of such grammar schools was not to provide a rounded education but to equip scholars for a career in the law or the church.

For 150 years the King Edward Grammar School was located in the old Guild Hall. Accommodation and facilities were limited, and the majority of students were day pupils. When the wooden Guild Hall burnt down in 1707, a newer, bigger building was raised on the same site, giving the school the opportunity to take more pupils, boarders as well as day pupils. The school was again rebuilt and enlarged in 1833, and the curriculum too was expanded, with less emphasis upon Latin grammar. There was now room for even more pupils who were, however, still restricted to being boys from Anglican families. However, during the course of the 19th century there developed the gradual recognition that girls too deserved an education beyond the rudimentary learning necessary to become good housewives, and the King Edward's High School for Girls was founded.

By the start of the 20th century, New Street had become a prime site for the expanding retailing and service industries in Birmingham, and there was pressure on the King Edward's School to sell its valuable land and relocate elsewhere. In 1937 it was decided to relocate the two schools to the leafy suburbs of Edgbaston and at the same time to take the opportunity to bring together the boys and girls schools on one site. The school was opened at its present site in 1947.

Turn left along the road, cross Pritchatts Road and keep ahead along Edgbaston Road to reach the Winterbourne Research Institute on your right.

Winterbourne House, built in 1902–04 by J.I. Ball, is one of the finest examples of a domestic residence built in the Arts and Crafts style. The house was surrounded by extensive gardens, a passion of the original owner J.S. Nettlefold. He devoted much time, effort and money to collecting and cultivating unusual plants and creating exotic settings for them, including a Japanese garden complete with tea-house and bridge. The house was eventually sold to the university, who used it to form the basis of their Botanical Gardens. Today this is the Winterbourne Research Institute, part of the university's botany department, where an extensive programme of plane breeding is undertaken. The original Winterbourne House, although modified, still forms the heart of the institute.

Continue along Edgbaston Road, lined with halls of residence for the university. Cross Somerset Road and keep ahead to where

Edgbaston Road bends right, then turn left through bollards on to a path leading to a lake. This open area, with halls of residence on the top of the slope in front, is called the Vale. Turn right and walk anti-clockwise around the lake.

In 1951 Birmingham University had the highest proportion of students living in private lodgings of any provincial university in England. It had only one hall of residence, and lodgings in the immediate vicinity of the university were hard to come by. Seven acres of land had been given to the university in 1949 to build more halls of residence, and another 110 acres were acquired in 1955, mainly here, in the area now known as the Vale.

In 1956 the Vale was a mature parkland. On the top of the slope were three large 19th-century villas with extensive gardens, while behind those was a grassy open sward planted with clumps of mature trees, descending a gentle slope to a low-lying boggy meadow. Architects Sir Hugh Casson and Neville Conder were commissioned to transform the area into a purpose-built student village. However, they were not content to simply build student accommodation, but wished instead to blend that accommodation into a landscaped environment, reminiscent of the great county estates of the 18th century but transplanted into the centre of a sprawling city.

Purpose-built halls of residence in the Vale.

The old villas were demolished, and three blocks of halls of residence were raised, one a 22-storey tower block, the other two more low-rise. The grounds of the villas were extensively recontoured to hide the halls from the road and the houses of Edgbaston. The slope behind was replanted and landscaped and a lake created in the boggy bottom. The new parkland, a triumph of 18th-century revivalism, was intended as a companion-piece to the grounds of Edgbaston Hall, on the opposite side of the road. Although the subsequent building of further halls and blocks of student flats around the edge of the Vale has somewhat diluted Casson and Conders's original design, the Vale can still be appreciated as a visionary piece of residential building.

At the end of the lake cross a bridge and turn right for 50 yards to a road. Turn left down the road and follow it back to Edgbaston Road. Turn right along Edgbaston Road, shortly turning right into Somerset Road. At the first crossroads, turn left into Farquhar Road. At a mini roundabout, keep ahead down Vincent Drive, the Birmingham Research Park on your left. Follow Vincent Drive past the Queen Elizabeth Hospital.

The Queen Elizabeth Hospital was opened in 1938 and was home to the university medical school. It was the largest medical development in Britain at the time and housed many related medical disciplines on one unified campus. Cost constraints forced the architects to eschew any unnecessary ornamentation, and to go instead for a design based on one massive tower, with two smaller associated blocks. The overall effect is somewhat austere.

At a roundabout at the top of the hill, cross the zebra crossing on the left, and then turn left down the side road for 30 yards to return to University Station.

Walk 12

Bourneville: the creation of a garden suburb

George Cadbury was a deeply religious man, a devout Quaker who believed in practical Christianity and who was deeply concerned with improving the social conditions of the working class. When George and his brother Richard relocated their chocolate factory to Bourneville, he set about putting his beliefs into practice. The factory was as environmentally friendly as possible, and it was surrounded by a model village, created to provide the factory workers with good-quality housing in a pleasant setting. Not only houses, but a school, civic centre, shops and churches were all built as part of Cadbury's ambitious plan.

Unlike the founders of similar ventures, such as Lord Leverhulme's Port Sunlight, Cadbury was not paternalistic, but believed instead in empowering his workers to run their own community once he had built it. Initially the houses were to be sold, but when it became apparent that many workers could not afford to buy their own homes, the Bourneville Village Trust was set up to offer rented properties at sensible prices on long leases. The Bourneville estate was laid out in 1894 by surveyor Alfred Walker, with wide roads and houses in groups of four or less, surrounded by gardens, all designed to provide maximum air and light in the estate. The following year William Alexander Harvey was appointed chief architect for the estate. This was a bold decision, since Harvey was only 20 and was inexperienced, certainly for a project of this size. In the next

Bust of George Cadbury, in a niche in the wall of the Friends Meeting House.

five years Harvey built the first 300 houses in Bourneville. By 1914 the original Bourneville estate, bordered by Mary Vale Road to the south and Raddlebarn Road in the north, had nearly 900 homes and was largely finished. That original estate remains little altered today, a monument to the vision and philanthropy of George Cadbury.

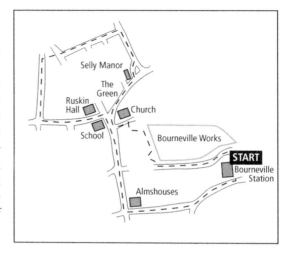

Start

Bourneville Station. There is a frequent train service from New Street station.

From the ticket office side of Bourneville Station, exit on to the road.

When Cadbury's relocated to Bourneville in 1878, the station was already here, primarily a freight station on the Great Western Railway. The GWR was of major importance to Cadbury's in distributing their products, and a spur line was built running through the factory and connecting it to the main line. However, the GWR was quick to realise the potential business generated by tourism, and heavily promoted the 'Borderlands of Birmingham', such as the Clent and Lickey Hills and Stratford-on-Avon, as destinations for day trips. The Cadbury philosophy encouraged its workers to get out into the fresh air of the countryside and also encouraged the growing trend for holidays by the seaside. Bourneville Station soon became the starting point for workers and their families bound for the coast at resorts such as Weston-super-Mare.

Turn left along the road, the factory on your right.

In 1824 John Cadbury had diversified his business from roasting cocoa beans to manufacturing chocolate as well, an experimental step which was to lead to the country's foremost chocolate empire. Cadbury was a pre-eminent citizen, the last chairman of the Street Commissioners, the ruling body of Birmingham before the Council was created, and an Overseer of the Poor. A devout Quaker, he was very concerned with the well-being of Birmingham's working class. As well as campaigning for a number of social reforms, a major concern of his was to improve living conditions by reducing the atmospheric pollution caused by the burgeoning industry in the city. When Cadbury relocated his business to Bridge Street in 1847 he put many of his beliefs into practice. His new factory had a chimney which did not give off smoke, he was the first factory-owner in Birmingham to enforce half-day closing on Saturdays, he gave his workforce an additional half-day off each week in the summer months and he encouraged his workers to attend evening classes. This philosophy of care for the well-being of the workforce and the environment was carried on by his sons, and it has remained a guiding principle of the Cadbury business ever since.

In 1878 the lease on the Bridge Street factory expired. The company was now run by John Cadbury's two sons, George and Richard, and they relocated the factory to a greenfield site on the outskirts of Selly Oak. Initially the factory was called Bournebrook, after a Georgian manor house that stood nearby, but the name was soon changed to Bourneville, since it was felt that the French connotations would make the product more marketable. The factory's output was initially mainly cocoa with some chocolate, but by 1880 it was increasingly diversifying into manufacturing confectionery. As well as servicing an ever-growing domestic market, exports became an increasingly important source of

Pavilion erected in 1902 to commemorate the Coronation of Edward VII.

sales. The first Cadbury's chocolates were exported to Australia in the late 1880s, with the rest of the empire soon following. The famous Cadbury's Dairy Milk was launched in 1904 and was followed 10 years later by Milk Tray. At its peak, 2,000 bars of chocolate an hour were being manufactured.

Over the 130 years it has been in existence the Bourneville factory has evolved almost beyond recognition. Very little of the original 1878 factory can still be seen, although the splendid classical façade from 1908 remains. But although the factory has changed, the practical application of the Cadbury's vision is all around us as we walk through the suburb they created.

Continue along the road, passing the Social Club on your left, to a zebra crossing.

The buildings of the Social Club are a much later addition to the Bourneville factory complex. Although the factory built by George and Richard Cadbury made provision for the recreational needs of the workforce by providing sporting facilities, a social club was not seen as necessary. Cadbury's vision was that the factory and the surrounding estate where the workers lived was an integrated whole, and that social functions should take place outside work, in the community not in the factory.

Cross the zebra crossing and keep ahead along an enclosed footpath, signed 'Cadbury World'.

On the right, as part of the factory, were swimming baths provided for the use of the workforce. There had been public baths in Birmingham since 1851, which were not primarily swimming pools but which contained closets where the general public could have a hot bath, a luxury impossible in crowded terraced housing with no bathrooms. Although the housing provided for the Cadbury workforce was affluent by comparison to that most factory workers enjoyed, the Cadbury brothers incorporated a baths for their workforce into their factory. Unlike most municipal baths, the main emphasis was on swimming pools for recreational swimming, and although some facilities for bathing were part of the initial baths these were little used and were soon removed.

Follow the footpath past a recreation field on your left.

This is the Men's Recreation Field, opened in 1896. Football, cricket, hockey and bowls are all played here in season. The Cadbury brothers were anxious to provide for the physical and spiritual well-being of their workers, and viewed the opportunity for sport as a vital part of this. Unusually for the time, the provision of a sports field was built into the plans for the factory as an integral part of the design. The ornate pavilion was erected six years later, in 1902, to commemorate the Coronation of Edward VII.

Continue along the footpath until water is reached on your right.

This stream is the Bourne Brook. It was here long before the factory and was originally called Trout Stream. Technically, the stream is a 'bourne', a stream that is dry for some seasons of the year, and the 'Bourne' was taken as the first half of the name for the area. On the far side of the water are the tracks of the Bourneville Railway, a narrow gauge railway that ran for five miles around the site.

Follow the footpath to the gates of a car park. Do not enter the car park but turn right to reach an access road. Cross the zebra crossing and turn left. Follow the footpath past a church to the road.

The Church of St Francis of Assisi is Bourneville's parish church. It is actually two connected buildings. To the north, nearest the Green, is the mission church, a simple, Romanesque design, with an arched entrance behind columns, built in 1913. Adjoining it is the more impressive main church, to the same Romanesque

Church of St Francis of Assisi.

design but laid out as a basilica with side aisles. The church was designed by W. Alexander Harvey who, although he ceased to be official architect for the estate in 1905, returned many times to design individual buildings. The Church of St Francis was built to accommodate the needs of Bourneville's non-Quaker workers and was originally conceived on a far grander scale than finally occurred. Although the mission church was opened in 1913, the main building was delayed for a further 12 years, finally opening its doors in 1925. A cloistered garden linking the two buildings at the rear was not finally built until 1937, and a planned bell tower was never built.

Turn right up the main road, and in 50 yards turn right into Sycamore Road.

The parade of shops was built between 1905–08 as an entity, in a tastefully executed mock-Tudor style by George Cadbury, the driving force behind the Bourneville Estate, and although it was built in the 20th century he was keen to give it the air of a much older and longer-established community. None of the shops here sell alcohol, nor is there a public house anywhere on the Bourneville estate. Quakers believe in total abstinence from alcohol, and George Cadbury insisted upon this for his workforce. The prohibition on the sale of alcohol on the estate is maintained by its inhabitants to the present day: when Tesco attempted to open a store in Bourneville in 2006, which would sell alcohol as part of its product range, it provoked vehement protests from the local community, who saw such a move as altering the essential nature of the area. Unusually, Tesco bowed to the wishes of the local population

The Rest House, paid for by donations from Bourneville workers.

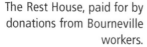

and at the time of writing have withdrawn their application for a liquor licence.

Cross the road at the zebra crossing in front of the shops, and keep ahead on to the green. Keep ahead to the Rest House.

Alfred Walker aimed to create a rustic, rural impression in his design of Bourneville village, and the green lay at the heart of his 1894 layout. It was planned as an open green, flanked by the church and the Quaker meeting house, and with other civic buildings such as the school and the community centre facing it. The Rest House was added later, in 1913. It was paid for by donations from Cadbury workers to commemorate the silver wedding of George and Elizabeth Cadbury, a reflection of the esteem Cadbury was held in by his workforce. The design, by W. Alexander Harvey, is based upon a 16th-century Somerset yarn house, where yarn was separated prior to weaving.

Continue across the Green to the Friends Meeting House.

The Meeting House is central to any Quaker community. Quaker religious meetings do not rely upon a formal service officiated by a priest, but rather allow for a meeting of the whole community, where any member of the congregation can speak when inspired to. The interior of this meeting house is

The Friends Meeting House.

simple, a large undivided room dominated by a mock hammer beam roof. The meeting house was built by Alexander Harvey in 1905, and was inspired by the First Church of Christ Scientist in Manchester. In a niche in the southern wall, facing on to the Green, is a bust of George Cadbury, sculpted in 1924 by Francis Wood.

On the opposite side of the main road is Ruskin Hall, built between 1902 and 1905 by Alexander Harvey as the village institute. George Cadbury was concerned that the inhabitants of his estate should have a secular community centre, as well as a religious centre, where they could gather for civic functions, entertainments, community meetings and the like. The hall includes a large assembly room, smaller meeting rooms and a library. Typically, Cadbury's 'village hall' was built to be aesthetically pleasing as well as functional. In keeping with several of the major buildings in Bourneville, the hall was deliberately designed to look older than it was, with grand peaked gables and the occasional mock-Tudor adornment. Ruskin Hall was built with a second purpose in mind, namely, to be a national memorial to John Ruskin, the intellectual powerhouse behind the Arts and Crafts Movement that was so important in Birmingham (see Walk 10). The influence of the Arts and Crafts movement can be seen in the layout and buildings of the Bourneville estate.

From the Meeting House, cross the green diagonally, leaving the

Ruskin Hall, built as the village institute.

Rest House on your right and passing in front of the Day Continuation School.

Education was an important part of George Cadbury's philosophy. He was convinced that if the working classes could be provided with ready access to education, and especially education with a practical application, not only would their lives be enriched but they would also spend their time and money on fruitful activities and not squander them on alcohol. The plans for Bourneville village stipulated that each house would cover no more than a quarter of the plot it was built upon, the rest being garden, and from the very outset gardening skills among the tenants were encouraged and increased through evening classes. Initially those classes were held in the school and other buildings, but as the demand for further education increased a dedicated building was required. The Day Continuation School was built in 1925.

Keep ahead to the road, and turn right to continue along Sycamore Road to cross Maple Road.

Another example of George Cadbury's desire to make his new estate appear far older and longer established than it was can be seen on the corner of Maple Road. Selly Manor was a mediaeval manor house that originally stood at the heart of Selly Oak, then a separate village two miles north of here. When the manor was threatened with demolition in the early 20th century, Cadbury arranged for it to be carefully deconstructed and moved here, into the heart of his new Bourneville estate. Selly Manor was rebuilt by Alexander Harvey between 1912 and 1916, partly from the original mediaeval materials, and partly using modern materials carefully integrated into the original design.

The old and the new are seamlessly blended in Harvey's construction, and to the untutored eye it is difficult to detect what is original and what is not. Three gabled half-timbered wings face out on to Sycamore Road. The left-hand gable, with its projecting first-floor 'jetty', is the original 15th-century building. The middle gable is partially reconstructed, while the right-hand gable is totally rebuilt, but as a faithful copy of the 16th-century original. The brick chimney stack, with its decorated chimneys, is original, an early 17th-century addition to the original hall. The gabelled porch, opening on to Maple Road, had been demolished by the time the manor was moved, and it was reconstructed by Harvey using an old watercolour painting as the pattern. The porch leads into the original hall, the middlemost of the three gables seen from Sycamore Road, dating from 1600.

Next to Selly Manor, just a little further along Maple Road, is Minworth

Selly Manor, moved from Selly Oak and re-erected in Bourneville.

Greaves, a hall dating from the 15th century and moved to this spot in 1929. Far more of this building has been reconstructed, with only the wall frames and cross beams being original.

Continue along Sycamore Road.

The houses along this stretch of road all date from 1902, some of the original homes built by Alexander Harvey for Cadbury's workers. Although the estate was built as a piece and over the space of only a few years, it avoids uniformity. The houses along Sycamore Road show a wide variety of sizes and styles, from elaborately gabled Dutch-style buildings, through grand three-storey Victorian town houses to simple semis. Three-quarters of each plot of land was originally garden and, although some of this has subsequently been eroded by garages and so on, the impression of light and greenery still pervades the area.

Bear left with the road, passing a small green on your right, to enter Willow Road.

This small triangle was deliberately laid out to resemble a village green, and thus reinforce the impression of a long-established community. The war memorial that stands on the Green commemorates the workers of Bourneville

Workers' houses in Bourneville.

who died in World War One. Although the Cadbury family, as Quakers, refused to fight in the armed services, killing one's fellow man being totally contrary to their religious beliefs, many of their employees were not Quakers and joined the forces. Some of these were among the 12,400 Birmingham men who died in that conflict. While the Cadburys were not prepared to kill, they made a positive contribution to the war effort, increasing production to supply food for the troops.

Continue along Willow Road and then turn left into Acacia Road.

The northern boundary of the original Bourneville estate was one street north of here. The quiet roads we are walking through were laid out in the first decade of the 20th century. The majority of the houses were designed either by W. Alexander Harvey or by H. Bedford Taylor, who took over from Harvey as chief

A deliberate re-creation of a village green in Bourneville.

architect to the estate in 1905. Taylor was the architect responsible for the parade of shops we have seen. These two men, Harvey and Taylor, between them gave Bourneville its distinctive character. Instead of building an anonymous housing estate, they created attractive suburban streets lined with individualistic homes.

Continue along Acacia Road, passing Stocks Wood on your left.

This small patch of woodland, now managed by the Bourneville Trust, is a tiny survivor of the great Forest of Arden. None of its trees are older than 150 years, but they are the descendants of those which stood here in mediaeval times.

Cross Maple Road and keep ahead to reach Linden Road. Cross Linden Road and keep ahead along an alley. At the far end, turn left along the road. Continue along the road to reach a junction with Woodbrooke Road.

On the corner on the right is St George's Court, built in 1925 as flats for single professional women. The Cadbury family were ahead of their time in many ways, one of which was recognising the importance of women in the business world. At a time when the traditional view was that 'a woman's place was in the home', and that females if they worked at all would only be employed in low-grade jobs, the Cadburys realised not only the contribution women could make to the higher levels of business, but that professional women could well be single and require a place of their own to live.

Turn left along Woodbrooke Road.

On the left is a range of almshouses, built in the early part of the 20th century. Providing accommodation for the needy of the estate was always a concern for George Cadbury, and a little later in the walk we will see an earlier almshouse complex built by him. These later almshouses continue the tradition Cadbury started.

Follow Woodbrooke Road out to the main road

On the right-hand side of the road as you approach the junction is Bourneville Junior School, built by Harvey in 1905. When Cadbury built Bourneville, it was conceived as a total community, not just accommodation for workers. Two schools were built, the junior school and an adjoining infants' school. As with all Bourneville's civic buildings, the schools were designed to be aesthetically

Bourneville Junior School.

pleasing as well as functional. The school is the tallest building on the Green, subliminally highlighting the importance of education in a community. The imposing main building for the junior school has a feeling of mass and solidity, with its turreted roof and oriel window, again highlighting the importance of education. On the other hand, the classrooms behind are lighter in design, airier and more open. While the main hall reminds the community of the school's importance, the pupils learn in a more friendly and less intimidating atmosphere. Just around the corner, facing the main road, the infants' school, built five years later, is a far simpler design and even more accommodating to younger pupils.

Cross the main road in front of the green and then turn right down the road, passing the entrance to Cadbury World on your left and keeping ahead.

Entrance to the Infants' School.

On the right is Bourneville Park, a comparatively small area of open land along the banks of the Bourne Brook. The provision of open areas that would provide fresh air and recreation for working men was vital in many areas of inner-city Birmingham. It was far less important in Bourneville, due to the very leafy and green nature of the estate George Cadbury had created, as well as the large recreation grounds provided around the factory itself. Nevertheless pockets of open ground were maintained to further enhance the facilities of Bourneville.

Cross Bourneville Lane and keep ahead.

173

The face of the Bourneville Factory, built in 1878.

The high wall on your left surrounds the Ladies' Recreation Ground. As we have seen, with the provision of St George's Court, George Cadbury recognised and valued the contribution made by women in his factory, and very unusually for the late Victorian era he thought that women as well as men should have sports facilities. In the interests of propriety the facilities for the two sexes were kept separate, and the women's recreation ground was further protected from prying eyes by being laid out behind the high protective wall of the former Bournebrook Hall. This large Georgian mansion, long since demolished, was owned by William Martin, half of the architectural firm of Martin & Chamberlain who produced so many of Birmingham's civic buildings.

Turn left into Mary Vale Road.

On the left are the Bourneville Almshouses, built in 1897 and given to the community by George Cadbury. They were designed by architects Ewen and Harper, and consist of a series of semi-detached cottages, facing ranges of terraced cottages across two grassy quadrangles. Along the road are continuous terraces, broken by arches and the imposing gatehouse. The total complex is single storey, and each cottage was designed to house a single occupant. Unlike many almshouses, these were mixed sex and were built to provide shelter for members of the community who could not afford to look after themselves.

Bourneville almshouses, built in 1897 for the poor of the estate.

Mary Vale Road was the southern limit of the original Bourneville Estate and the first houses of the estate were built along here between 1895 and 1900, largely to designs by Alexander Harvey. Many of the houses on the left side of the road, beyond the almshouses, are from that era. The houses on the opposite side of the road are an interesting contrast to the houses we have seen until now. These solid terraces, built in the early 20th century, are not part of Cadbury's Bourneville Estate. The whole south side of the street is one long terrace, each unit with its standardised bay windows and tunnel-like entries leading to the back yards. Although they are good solid properties that have undoubtedly stood the test of time, they lack the individuality and aesthetic appeal that George Cadbury went to such lengths to introduce into the homes he built for his workers.

Follow the Vale to where it crosses the railway. Immediately before the railway bridge, turn left down on to the platform of Bourneville Station.

Printed in Great Britain
by Amazon

60023986R00102